THAILAND
in Pictures

VGS

Stacy Taus-Bolstad

Lerner Publications Company

Contents

Website address: www.lernerbooks.com

Lerner Publications Company
A division of Lerner Publishing Group
241 First Avenue North
Minneapolis, MN 55401 U.S.A.

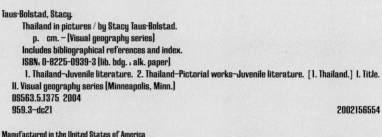

Library of Congress Cataloging-in-Publication Data

Taus-Bolstad, Stacy.
    Thailand in pictures / by Stacy Taus-Bolstad.
        p.   cm. – (Visual geography series)
    Includes bibliographical references and index.
    ISBN: 0-8225-0939-3 (lib. bdg. : alk. paper)
        1. Thailand–Juvenile literature. 2. Thailand–Pictorial works–Juvenile literature. [1. Thailand.] I. Title.
    II. Visual geography series (Minneapolis, Minn.)
    DS563.5.T375 2004
    959.3–dc21   2002156554

Manufactured in the United States of America
1 2 3 4 5 6 - JR - 09 08 07 06 05 04

INTRODUCTION

Located in Southeast Asia, Thailand is a mostly rural country that is home to more than 62 million people. Thailand has been nicknamed the Land of Smiles because of the friendly nature of its people. The Thai people are famous for their hospitality to strangers and their easygoing natures. They are also strong-minded and proud of their culture. They have long been united by language, religion, and respect for the country's monarchy.

Thailand's official name, Muang Thai, means "land of the free," and Thailand has a long history of independence. From the earliest emergence of a unified Thai kingdom in the thirteenth century, the country has maintained its independence. Even when European powers colonized most parts of Asia between the sixteenth and nineteenth centuries, Thai kings managed to avoid foreign domination.

Many cultures have contributed to Thailand's culture. Trade with India, China, and Sri Lanka—and later with European countries—introduced ideas and cultural practices that have influenced Thai religions, social systems, and technologies.

Thailand has been a constitutional monarchy since 1932, when the country introduced a new constitution that established two houses of legislature. While the constitution greatly reduced the monarch's power, the Thai people remained steadfast in their respect for the royal family. The government has undergone many changes in leadership since the introduction of democracy in the 1930s, but the king remains a constant figure in the Thai political arena.

Under the new system, however, the nation's leaders have changed frequently, and the country has had little political stability. Although its leadership has not been consistent or enduring, Thailand has managed to make steady economic progress. During the 1950s and 1960s, Thailand worked hard to modernize businesses and transportation systems. Banks and businesses grew, and by the 1980s the country had joined the global economy.

In the late 1980s and early 1990s, foreign investment helped Thailand shift its emphasis from agricultural to industrial production.

Major exports included textiles, rubber, plastics, and seafood. Low taxes and a large, educated workforce encouraged Thai and foreign business leaders to invest billions of dollars in the Thai economy. Economic experts even predicted that by 2020 Thailand would be one of the top ten economic systems in the world.

The boom didn't last, however. In 1997 the baht, the Thai monetary unit, lost its value amidst an Asia-wide economic crisis. As the stock market crashed, inflation rates soared. Thailand underwent a huge recession, and many people lost their jobs and their fortunes. Many young people left the cities to move back to their rural villages, where they returned to farming.

These economic woes also created social problems for the country. As Thailand industrialized, the gap between rich people and poor people widened. Under the developing economy, wealthy business owners exploited the country's natural resources. While a few rich families grew richer, many other families lost their livelihood, becoming more impoverished than ever before. At the beginning of the twenty-first century, estimates showed that wealthy Thai families earned nearly 15 times more than the country's poorest families. And as more poor people were forced to move to the cities to look for work, family problems, prostitution, and drug addiction soared.

Thailand is working to rebuild its economy. The lack of strong leadership, however, has slowed the country's recovery. Other problems have also contributed to the sluggish revival. The country's communication and transportation systems remain largely underdeveloped. And unregulated urban development has led to deforestation, pollution, and other serious environmental problems.

Despite the nation's difficulties, Thai leaders remain optimistic. They point to the country's well-educated citizens, its history of economic growth, and to various government modernization efforts as indicators of a promising future for their nation.

THE LAND

Thailand occupies 198,116 square miles (513,118 square kilometers) of territory, about twice the size of the state of Wyoming. Lying in the center of Southeast Asia, Thailand includes a narrow strip that juts southward along a 550-mile-long (885-km) portion of the Malay Peninsula, which Thailand shares with Myanmar (formerly Burma) and Malaysia.

Thailand's border with Myanmar extends beyond the peninsula to the west and northwest. Laos and Cambodia lie along the nation's eastern boundary. The Gulf of Thailand, an arm of the South China Sea, forms the country's southeastern edge. The Andaman Sea—part of the Indian Ocean—stretches along the western coast of peninsular Thailand.

Several islands lie off the shores of Thailand. Phuket is the largest Thai island in the Andaman Sea, and Ko Samui is one of the larger islands in the Gulf of Thailand. Many Thai islands contain untapped mineral resources, such as tin and granite. They also have potential for tourism because of their picturesque beaches.

Topography

Thailand extends almost 1,100 miles (1,770 km) from north to south, and it is about 500 miles (805 km) across at its widest point. The nation's territory falls into four topographical regions—the northern mountains, the central plain, the Khorat Plateau, and the southern peninsula.

The northern mountain ranges, which run in a north-south direction, compose about one-fourth of the nation's territory. These peaks lie along Thailand's borders with Myanmar to the west and Laos to the northeast. Elevations are the highest in the west, and the tallest point in the country, Doi Inthanon at 8,514 feet (2,595 meters) above sea level, stands in the extreme northwestern part of the nation.

Rivers flow between the mountains, and farmers raise crops in the steep river valleys. The rivers wash away sand and mud from the mountainsides and eventually deposit the fertile soil in the central plain. The mountains once provided plenty of evergreens and teak trees for logging.

Expansion of agriculture, however, has led to deforestation and has caused timber shortages.

The most populous region in the country is the central plain, which extends almost 300 miles (480 km) northward from the Gulf of Thailand to the foothills of the northern mountains. The Bilauktaung Mountains form the plain's western boundary, and the Phetchabun Mountains define part of the region's eastern edge.

The terrain of the central plain is very flat, and a large river system—the Chao Phraya and its tributaries—dominates the landscape. This waterway irrigates the soil, making the plain a fertile agricultural area that yields large harvests of rice. An extensive network of canals (called *khlongs*) provides additional irrigation and access to river traffic.

The square-shaped Khorat Plateau is located in northeastern Thailand. The Phetchabun Mountains border the plateau on the west, and the Phanom Dong Rak range marks the plateau's southern boundary. The Mekong River flows along the northern and eastern limits of the plateau.

Composing about one-third of the nation's land area, the Khorat Plateau is the least fertile area of the country. Seasonal droughts and rains make farming difficult. In addition, the porous, sandy soil makes irrigation difficult on the plateau. Nevertheless, Thai farmers grow rice in the areas of the plateau that can be irrigated.

Thailand's southern peninsular region, part of the Malay Peninsula, contains a portion of the Bilauktaung Mountains. The highest point in the peninsular section of this chain is Doi Luang at 7,201 feet (2,195 m) above sea level. The southern peninsula has narrow coastal plains, where farmers cultivate rice, rubber trees, and coconuts.

Rice is Thailand's staple crop. This rice paddy in the central plain is just one of thousands in Thailand.

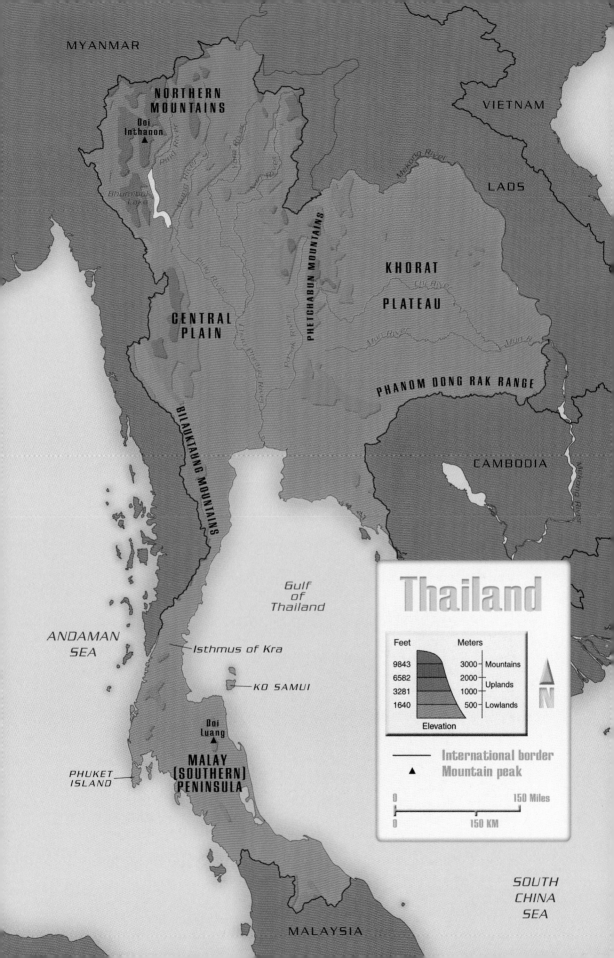

The section of the peninsula that Thailand and Myanmar share varies from 30 to 150 miles (48 to 241 km) in width. The narrowest point is along the Isthmus of Kra. Thai engineers and government leaders have considered building a canal for shipping across the isthmus (a narrow strip of land that links two larger land areas). Numerous obstacles, particularly the lack of financial resources and political instability, continue to hamper this long-awaited project.

Rivers

Thailand's main river is the Chao Phraya. Flowing southward through the central plain, it provides ample water for the region's many rice fields. The khlongs that were built to carry water from the river to the fields also serve as a transportation system and provide a fishing ground for the large population that lives in the area. Bangkok, Thailand's capital city, lies on the Chao Phraya 20 miles (32 km) upstream from the Gulf of Thailand.

Four rivers—the Ping, Wang, Yom, and Non—are tributaries that begin in the northern mountains and feed the Chao Phraya. The Pasak, which runs parallel to the Phetchabun Mountains in the center of the country, also links up with the Chao Phraya River.

The Chi and Mun Rivers form the main drainage system on the Khorat Plateau. These waterways run eastward into the Mekong River,

The Mekong River forms the long border between Thailand and neighboring countries Laos and Cambodia.

Passenger boats zip across the Chao Phraya River near Bangkok.

which winds through Laos, Cambodia, and Vietnam before emptying into the South China Sea.

In addition to the major waterways, Thailand has many short rivers, several small, widely scattered lakes, and a few reservoirs. The plentiful rains that fall during the wet season swell the rivers, providing irrigation for rice and other crops and renewing the nation's water transportation system.

Flooding and mudslides are common during **monsoon season** in Thailand. These strong seasonal winds often bring fierce storms to the region.

Climate

Monsoons (seasonal winds) determine Thailand's three seasons. In late May and June, a monsoon from the southwest starts to blow over the country, bringing rain from the Indian Ocean. With the rains comes a hot, wet summer season, which continues until October. Temperatures during this period average 90°F (32°C). The summer monsoon carries 90 percent of the country's annual rainfall. About 60 inches (152 centimeters) of rain fall each year in the northern mountains and in the central plains. The Khorat Plateau receives about 50 inches (127 cm), and the southern peninsula gets more than 100 inches (254 cm) of rainfall annually.

Winds blow from the opposite direction in November, when the northeast monsoon arrives, beginning Thailand's cool, dry winter. Air currents sweep southward across Asia and blow across the Gulf of Thailand. The monsoon picks up moisture as it crosses the gulf and brings rain to the Malay Peninsula. This moisture accounts for the higher precipitation levels in the southern peninsula, which receives rain during most of the year. The winter air is cool, and temperatures in Thailand range from 50° to 80°F (10° to 27°C).

The country's hot, dry spring begins in March and lasts until May. Temperatures during this season are usually in the nineties but sometimes soar over 100°F (38°C).

Natural Resources

Thailand's mineral resources include tin, zinc, coal, lignite (brown coal), lead, and limestone. The country also mines gemstones such as rubies, sapphires, and zircons. Thailand contains an estimated 516 million barrels of oil reserves, most located along the Gulf of Thailand. The country's largest natural gas field is at Bongkot, nearly 400 miles (644 km) south of Bangkok in the Gulf of Thailand.

The waters in and around Thailand provide both freshwater and saltwater fish, including shrimp, crab, and lobster. At the beginning of the twenty-first century, Thailand was the leading exporter of fishery commodities in the world.

Thailand's dwindling forests still provide some lumber, particularly teak, for the furniture and construction industries. Orchards produce tropical fruits such as pineapples, mangoes, and bananas, as well as several unusual varieties, such as durians and lychee.

Flora and Fauna

Thailand's vegetation is primarily tropical. The rain forests of the country's southern peninsula and the coast of the Gulf of Thailand are composed of mangrove, ebony, ironwood, and rattan palm trees. Rain forests thrive in warm, humid climates, which support the vegetation that grows beneath the forests' tallest trees. Stands of teak, redwood, oak, and evergreen are found in the northern mountains. The mountains fringing the Khorat Plateau are partially covered with evergreen forests.

Over the centuries, people living on the central plain gradually cut down the forests and planted rice fields, which they irrigated with water from the Chao Phraya and its tributaries. The Khorat Plateau's vegetation, on the other hand, has changed very little and supports sparse grasses, stunted trees, and thorny shrubs.

Gardenia

Bamboo, a giant variety of grass, grows throughout much of Thailand, especially in coastal areas. Orchids, gardenias, hibiscus, and many other flowering plants thrive in the country's tropical climate. Fruit trees—such as banana, mango, and coconut—also prosper in Thailand.

Tigers, leopards, rhinoceroses, Himalayan black bears, gibbons (tailless apes), and other animals live in the wilderness areas of the nation, especially in reserves such as Doi Inthanon National Park. Perhaps best known of all the Thai animals is the

More than one thousand varieties of orchids grow in Thailand. Farmers began raising the flowers for profit in the 1950s, but it wasn't until the 1980s that the industry blossomed. Since then, Thailand has become Southeast Asia's leading orchid exporter.

Siamese cat, which was introduced to European and North American countries in the nineteenth century. Water buffalo continue to be an important domestic animal for Thailand's farmers.

Water buffalo

Thailand's rivers and coastal waters host many varieties of fish and marine animals, including anchovies, mackerel, shrimp, and crab. Fish also swim in the waters of the flooded rice fields. Crocodiles inhabit the rivers and khlongs, and pythons and cobras are two of the many varieties of snakes found in the country. Thailand also has more than nine hundred varieties of birds, including parrots, storks, hornbills, and hawks.

Environmental Issues

Thailand's industrial growth has taken a heavy toll on the environment. While Thailand faces several environmental issues, pollution and the loss of wildlife are the two most significant environmental threats. Air pollution plagues Thailand's urban areas, particularly Bangkok. Toxic fumes from factories and traffic exhaust make the Thai capital one of the most air-polluted cities in the world. In addition, the country's recent economic problems have forced businesses to curb investment in costly but environmentally friendly programs, such as cleaner burning fuels, that would help alleviate the pollution problem.

Urban pollution is just one of Thailand's environmental problems, however. Thailand's wilderness is quickly disappearing. Farmers who live in the northern and western hills often cut and burn the natural mountainside vegetation to make new fields for their crops. After a few years of planting, the soil is no longer fertile, and the farmers move to new territory to begin the cycle of burning natural vegetation and planting crops again. This practice causes soil erosion, which is severely damaging the environment of northern Thailand. Estimates show that nearly three-quarters of Thailand was forested in the 1940s. Experts believe that in 2000, the figure had dropped to less than one-fifth.

Because of widespread deforestation, many plants and animals have lost their habitats. Thailand's industries also hurt certain animal populations. For example, Asian elephants were once trained to move timber from the northern mountain forests to rivers. While these great creatures once numbered in the hundreds of thousands across Asia, fewer than two thousand remain in Thailand's wilds. The list of threatened and endangered species grows each year. This list includes tigers, leopards, Asian elephants, and Himalyan black bears.

Asian elephants were once vital to the Thai logging industry. Due to vanishing habitat and poaching, they are endangered in Thailand and throughout Asia.

Tourism has proven to be both a blessing and a curse to Thailand's environment. The growing industry has brought in some much-needed revenue for its underdeveloped conservation and economic programs. More visitors, however, also mean more damage.

Since the 1960s, the Thai government has attempted to establish several conservation programs. In 1964 the government passed the Wild Animals Reservation and Protection Act to protect wild animals and to establish areas where hunting was not allowed. The act also identified several species that were near extinction. Other conservation efforts include Wildlife Fund Thailand in 1983 and the National Environmental Quality Act in 1992.

Some of these efforts have helped. Eighty national parks and thirty-two wildlife sanctuaries protect more than 850 species. Conservationists hope that better preservation programs and increased public awareness will save more of Thailand's wildlife from extinction. And in the late twentieth century, the Thai

ENDANGERED ANIMALS

Thailand has few laws protecting its endangered species. Because of its loose policies regarding the importation of animals—including endangered animals—Thailand has become a market for animals poached (illegally hunted) in Burma, Cambodia, and even Africa and South America. Bangkok in particular is sometimes known as the "wildlife supermarket of the world" because buyers go there to purchase rare and protected species, dead or alive.

government announced a twenty-year policy for environmental protection. However, rebuilding the country's industrial economy may prove to be an obstacle to improving its environmental quality.

Visit vgsbooks.com to find links to websites where you can learn about Thailand's wildlife, efforts to save endangered species, climate and current weather conditions, and cities, including Bangkok (Krung Thep).

Cities

Although Thailand is predominantly a rural country, people have migrated to the cities at a fast rate since the mid-1960s. Bangkok, known as Krung Thep in the Thai language, is the nation's capital and largest city, with a population of nearly ten million people. Located on the Chao Phraya River, Bangkok is the business, communication, transportation, and political hub of the nation. Khlongs once served as a major means of transportation for many people who lived in the center of the city. In the later part of the twentieth century, however, some of the khlongs were filled in to make room for new roads and for new housing.

Many rural people looking for work moved to Bangkok in the last half of the twentieth century, causing the city's population to skyrocket. This in turn strained the city's housing facilities and congested the underdeveloped roadways. City leaders have not guided the recent development of the urban landscape, however, and industrial, residential, and commercial buildings stand side by side. This intermingling has lead to pollution and health issues.

Nakhon Ratchasima (population 2.5 million) is an ancient walled town that lies on the Mun River. The site—also known as Khorat—is an important railroad junction and trading center for much of northeastern Thailand.

Chiang Mai (population 1.6 million) lies in the Ping River Valley in Thailand's northern mountains. The city's climate is cooler than most of Thailand, making it a popular vacation spot for tourists and locals alike. Chiang Mai and the surrounding area contain many historic buildings and temples, such as Wat Phra Singh—the region's most important Buddhist religious shrine. The city is also a commercial center for the north. Several ethnic groups from the surrounding mountains sell their handicrafts in the city's markets.

Situated on the bank of the Chao Phraya, Nonthaburi (population 394,000) lies just 13 miles (20 km) from Bangkok. The town boasts fruit orchards, flower plantations, and important historical temples.

Ubon Ratchathani (population 150,900), located near the junction of the Chi and Mun Rivers, is a commercial hub on the Khorat Plateau. Hat Yai (population 149,000) is the major trading center on Thailand's southern peninsula. Many Thai, as well as foreign tourists, visit Hat Yai while vacationing on the beaches of the southern peninsula.

Teeming Ratchada Road in **Bangkok** is similar to New York City's Times Square.

HISTORY AND GOVERNMENT

Distant ancestors of the people of Thailand settled in Southeast Asia about forty thousand years ago. These nomads hunted game and gathered edible plants.

Archaeological discoveries at Ban Chiang in the northeast and Ban Kao in the west reveal that people in the area practiced agriculture around 7000 B.C. Peas, beans, and eventually rice were the main crops that early Southeast Asians grew. Other evidence indicates that these groups developed pottery sometime around 3500 B.C. and metalworking around 2500 B.C.

Because agriculture provided an opportunity for a more settled way of life, ethnic groups became more distinct from one another. By the first century A.D., many of these clans had developed small villages and were planting rice as their main crop. The groups still hunted and gathered food in the forests and fished along the streams.

◯ Early Kingdoms

The Mon were one of the earliest ethnic groups to become politically organized in the region. In the first century A.D., they established the kingdom of Funan, which spread its influence over a large portion of Southeast Asia, eventually extending into what later became southern Vietnam, Cambodia, central Thailand, and the Malay Peninsula. In the fifth century, Mon merchants established a major commercial center on the Gulf of Thailand to serve ships that traveled between China and India. Contact between Indian traders and the local population brought India's Hindu religion to Southeast Asia. Hindu images and literature played a significant role in the development of Thai culture.

Funan began to decline in the sixth century. A new Mon kingdom, Dvaravati, rose on the edges of Thailand's central plain and began challenging Funan's power. Dvaravati drew its economic strength from the overland trade routes that went from what became present-day

21

Myanmar (formerly Burma), across Thailand, eastward to Cambodia, and northward to Laos.

By the end of the Funan era in the seventh century, ethnic groups with diverse backgrounds began to move into the area that became Thailand. Many of these immigrants came from Nanchao in the Yunnan area of southern China. Speaking languages collectively referred to as Thai, these people migrated to the central and northern areas of Thailand in the seventh century. These newcomers formed the basis of the modern Thai nation.

Just as they had welcomed Indian culture and the Hindu religion, the Mon were also receptive to monks from the island of Sri Lanka who came to Thailand in the eighth century. These monks were Buddhists, and they taught the Mon the ideas of Siddhartha Gautama, an Indian religious leader who had lived in the sixth century B.C. Buddhism quickly spread throughout Thailand.

Other empires began to take control of the area during this time. One of the most influential groups was the Khmer, which had its capital at Angkor in Cambodia. The Khmer king Yasovarman I, who reigned from 889 to 900, expanded his empire into northeastern and central Thailand. At his death, Yasovarman's realm included the Khorat Plateau.

Over the next few centuries, the Khmer Empire extended its control farther into Thailand. King Suryavarman I (1002–1050) conquered the Chao Phraya Valley, driving out the Mons. Suryavarman II further expanded the kingdom's control of the area, forcing the Mons deep into what eventually became Myanmar.

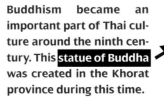
Buddhism became an important part of Thai culture around the ninth century. This statue of Buddha was created in the Khorat province during this time.

While the Khmer overcame the Mon militarily, they did not destroy the Hindu and Buddhist cultures, which existed together harmoniously. Instead, Hindu ideas—especially the concept of a divine king—influenced the Khmer, and soon the Khmer king adopted the characteristics of a Hindu god. Throughout their territory, the Khmer built stone palaces and temples in honor of their divine kings.

A system of roads that went from Angkor to provincial urban settlements helped hold the Khmer kingdom together through the twelfth century. The roads were elevated several feet above the plain to keep them from being flooded during the rainy season.

The Thai Emerge

Although the Khmer initially had authority over them, a new wave of Thai-speaking immigrants gained political and military strength as they continued to arrive from southern China. The Mon referred to the Thai speakers as Siamese. By 1238 they had defeated the Khmer and had set up their capital at Sukhothai. The Siamese established their first independent kingdom under King Phra Ruang and gave themselves the name Thai, which means "free people."

The fourth Siamese king, Rama Khamhaeng, began his forty-year reign in 1279. Under Rama Khamhaeng's leadership, trade with other kingdoms flourished. The Sukhothai kingdom developed a strong economy and a diverse culture. Rama Khamhaeng developed a Thai alphabet that was based on the Khmer writing system and ordered scholars to record his kingdom's history. In addition, he encouraged the continued spread of Buddhism during his reign.

Under Rama Khamhaeng's stable leadership, Sukhothai expanded to the south and west and became a more unified empire. After Rama Khamhaeng's death, however, other Thai states emerged and challenged the kingdom. By the middle of the fourteenth century, the kingdom of Sukhothai had greatly weakened.

"In the time of King Rama Khamhaeng this land of Sukhothai is thriving. There are fish in the water and rice in the fields."

—Rama Khamhaeng's "Inscription No. 1"

The Kingdom of Ayutthaya

As the Sukhothai Empire declined, many Thai migrated farther south along the Chao Phraya River. By the fourteenth century, several groups inhabited the fertile central plain, where they grew rice and established villages. One of these settlers, a leader named Rama Thibodi,

Many great feats of architecture, such as this **Ayutthayan temple,** were created during the prosperous Ayutthaya kingdom.

established a new dynasty (family of rulers) in 1350, with its capital at Ayutthaya. The kingdom of Ayutthaya overshadowed Sukhothai and had conquered it completely by 1378. Under Rama Thibodi and his successors, Ayutthaya grew to almost the size of present-day Thailand and lasted for more than four hundred years.

Rama Thibodi increased Hinduism's influence in his kingdom. Although he preserved many Thai legal customs, the king established a system of laws based on the Hindu belief in the unchanging law of nature. He clearly defined the roles of royalty and subjects, of men and women, and of slaves and free people. These laws were the first stage in the development of a detailed pattern of relationships in Thai society. A crime by a wealthy person against a farmer, for example, was punished less severely than the same crime committed by a farmer against a member of the nobility.

Despite the king's fondness for Hindu culture and ethics, Buddhism became the dominant religion of the kingdom. Another group of Buddhist monks from Sri Lanka came to the kingdom during this time, and Rama Thibodi allowed Buddhist religious leaders to establish monasteries and temples throughout the region.

While the kingdom developed internally, soldiers from Ayutthaya fought many battles with neighboring Khmer, Burmese, and Malays, as well as with other groups not under their control. In the late fourteenth and early fifteenth centuries, the kings of Ayutthaya focused on disputes with the Khmer from Angkor. Thai soldiers captured many

Khmer prisoners, and in 1431 Angkor was captured and destroyed. Ayutthaya forces also overcame the Malays on the southern peninsula as well as smaller Thai kingdoms near Chiang Mai.

Once its borders were more secure, Ayutthaya turned to internal affairs. King Trailok, who ruled from 1448 to 1488, instituted reforms that centralized the national administration. Previously, semi-independent local princes and governors had ruled many of the provinces of Ayutthaya. Local leaders were called to Ayutthaya and put in charge of the new governmental departments. They were required to live in the capital, where the king could easily oversee their work.

King Trailok also formed a rigid class system called *sakdi na*, which means "field power." All male Thai were given varying amounts of land according to their status. Slaves, craftspeople, and other subjects with little status received 10 acres (4 hectares) or less, while successful merchants and nobles were given as much as 4,000 acres (1,619 hectares). Women were not included in this arrangement. Under Trailok's system, a Thai man could change his rank and gain or lose sakdi na depending on whether he gained the favor or displeasure of the king.

To learn more about Thailand's history and up-to-date information on Thailand's government and current leaders, go to vgsbooks.com.

◯ European Contact

At the beginning of the sixteenth century, European explorers sailed their ships into the waters of Southeast Asia. The Portuguese—the first Europeans to make contact with the Thai—arrived in 1511, during the reign of Rama Thibodi II. After establishing a trading post at Melaka on the Malay Peninsula, the Portuguese sought to make a trade arrangement with the Thai government. Other European trading nations followed the example of the Portuguese, and Southeast Asia soon became a major commercial region, especially for rice, teak, and spices.

Meanwhile, the leaders of Ayutthaya turned their attention to deciding where the boundary line would be drawn with neighboring Burma. In 1549 Burmese forces invaded the kingdom but were quickly defeated. The Burmese briefly captured Ayutthaya in 1569, but the Thai king Naresuan defeated Burma's prince in a battle at Nong Sarai in 1593, ending these border disputes.

With its border secure, the Thai kingdom was able to improve its potential as a European trading outpost. By the early seventeenth century, the Dutch and the British had replaced the Portuguese as the most important European trading powers in Southeast Asia. Local rulers permitted foreign nations to open businesses and missions in Thailand. Some foreign traders were even given powerful positions in the kingdom's administration. The Thai sent an ambassador to the Netherlands in 1608, which marked the first visit by a Thai official to Europe.

European merchants soon intruded on the internal affairs of the Thai government. Interested in making large profits, the Europeans tried to shape events in the Thai kingdom for their own benefit. On one occasion, the Dutch sailed their warships into the Gulf of Thailand. This threat alarmed King Narai, who reigned from 1656 to 1688. By giving more trading influence to France—a newcomer in the commercial network—the king weakened Dutch influence in the area.

Relations between Thailand and European powers became strained. In 1688—after many maneuvers for power among Thai within the royal palace—a Thai group that opposed European influence took over the kingdom. The new rulers expelled most of the Europeans except for a few Dutch and Portuguese traders. The kingdom closed its ports to the Western world until 1826.

The Bangkok Era

Free of European interference, Thai rulers hoped for peace. Burma, the kingdom's neighbor to the west, had remained largely at peace since its defeat at Nong Sarai. But the Burmese resumed their border conflict with Thailand in 1760, when they attacked the city of Ayutthaya.

This sixteenth-century illustration shows boat traffic in the Gulf of Thailand. The gulf has served as a busy port for centuries.

In these initial attacks, however, the Burmese failed to overcome the city. Five years later, the Thai again had to defend themselves from their enemy to the west. In 1767, after a year of being under siege, Ayutthaya fell to Burmese forces. They destroyed buildings, written records, and works of art, and they killed or imprisoned thousands of Thai.

The Burmese left only small garrisons of their soldiers to protect conquered Thai territory. Phraya Taksin, a Thai general, led his troops against these Burmese detachments in late 1767, driving them out of the region.

Taksin chose Thonburi, a settlement on the Chao Phraya River, as his capital. After proclaiming himself king, Taksin forced rival Thai groups to come under his control. When Burmese troops attempted to retake Thai territory, Taksin's army turned them away. The king reigned until 1782, when rebel leaders overthrew him.

The rebels called on General Phraya Chakri to be the new Thai king. Chakri founded the Chakri dynasty, which continues into the twenty-first century. Each king of this dynasty took the ceremonial name Rama, after one of the principal Hindu gods. Chakri moved the capital from Thonburi to Bangkok, just across the Chao Phraya River. Under his rule, the Thai kingdom became known as Siam, and included pieces of territory from present-day Cambodia, Laos, and Malaysia.

By the nineteenth century, Europeans had colonized most of Southeast Asia and were pressuring Thai rulers to widen trade opportunities in Siam. Europeans sent trade representatives to Thai territory during Chakri's reign but failed to gain commercial access to the region. In 1826 the Thai kingdom and Great Britain signed the Burney Treaty, a trade and diplomatic agreement. In 1833 the United States received permission to

WHAT'S IN A NAME?

No one really knows where the name Siam originated. Some scholars believe it comes from Sanskrit—an ancient Indian language—and means "black." Others believe it's a variation of the word "Cham." Historians do know that as far back as the thirteenth century, the Khmer referred to the Thai people as Syamas. Neighboring kingdoms also used similar sounding names, including San and Siang, to refer to the Thai. When Europeans arrived in the area, they called the area Siam and the people Siamese. King Mongkut was the first ruler to officially use Siam as the country's name.

The Thai, however, have always called themselves Thai. During the nineteenth and twentieth centuries, as nationalist ideas spread through the kingdom, people began to demand a new name for their country. On May 8, 1939, the government officially changed the country's name from Siam to Thailand.

do business on the same limited basis as the British. By 1851, when King Mongkut (Rama IV) became Siam's monarch, the Thai realm had responded to the requests of foreign merchants for more open markets.

ANNA AND THE KING

In the Western world, King Mongkut is probably best known as the dancing monarch in the Hollywood movie *The King and I*. Many Thai, however, consider the movie offensive and dismiss it as pure fiction.

The person responsible for this image of the king, Anna Leonowens, was an English-woman who arrived in Bangkok in 1862 to serve as governess at Mongkut's royal court. She later wrote books about Thailand, *The English Governess at the Siamese Court* and *The Romance of the Harem*, which generated interest in Siam and its king.

From these works, Margaret Landon created the novel *Anna and the King of Siam* in 1944. In 1956 Landon's best-seller was made into a Broadway musical and a movie called the *King and I*. A new film version of the novel, *Anna and the King*, was released in 1999. Each version of the story has been banned in Thailand due to the historical inaccuracies and what the Thai perceive as a disrespectful portrayal of the monarchy.

◉ King Mongkut's Reign

Before he became king, Mongkut spent twenty-seven years in a Buddhist monastery where he studied scriptures, science, English, and European history. Mongkut saw value in learning European culture. He recognized, however, the threat that Western colonial nations posed to the independence of his kingdom.

The king protected his country by pitting foreign nations against one another. He achieved this goal in part by allowing many Western nations to have commercial opportunities in the kingdom. As a result, the king made it possible for colonizing nations to trade successfully in the kingdom without risking Siam's independence.

In 1855 Mongkut signed a treaty with Britain that broadened Thai trade activity, which had been outlined in the 1826 agreement. This new document gave the British merchants the right to buy and sell goods directly, without using Thai go-betweens. In addition, the Thai government reduced the heavy taxes that it had previously placed on imports.

British merchants began marketing Thai rice, teak, and tin in world commercial centers, and the Thai bought British manufactured goods, especially cloth, in exchange. Similar treaties were drawn up with the United States, France, and Portugal.

An elderly King Mongkut poses for a photograph with his young son, Prince Chulalongkorn.

Mongkut welcomed what he judged to be the positive influences of Western commerce on his country. The king encouraged his subjects to study science and European languages with the Christian missionaries who had accompanied the traders to the kingdom. Mongkut ordered a printing press to be set up in Bangkok, and soon a royal newspaper was published.

King Chulalongkorn's Reforms

When Mongkut died in 1868, his son Chulalongkorn (Rama V) became king. He continued his father's reforms. Chulalongkorn gradually reduced the number of slaves in order to avoid disrupting labor patterns by changing them too quickly. By 1905 the king had eliminated slavery, and debt slavery had also been phased out. Chulalongkorn reformed the tax system so that Thai citizens contributed money rather than labor to the government. The king also reorganized the sakdi na system. Instead of gaining control of parcels of land as payment for service, government workers and other laborers received salaries.

Among other reforms, Chulalongkorn tried to start a public education system for children in the kingdom. He sponsored the construction of new roads and a railroad network. The king took steps to curb the use of opium (an addictive drug made from opium poppies)—one of the kingdom's goods that was traded with European nations.

Despite expanded trade practices, Great Britain, and later France, continued to pressure the kingdom for territory. To prevent colonization by these nations, Chulalongkorn attempted to satisfy them by giving them outlying portions of Thai-controlled land.

In 1893 the Thai kingdom surrendered territory east of the Mekong River (in what is present-day Laos), as well as the western portion of Cambodia, to the French. In 1909 Great Britain, which was pressuring the Thai from colonies in Burma and Malaya, gained control of Thai areas on the Malay Peninsula. By partially satisfying the Europeans' desire for land, Chulalongkorn enabled most of the Thai kingdom to remain independent.

King Chulalongkorn *(seated, center)* **instituted many reforms during his reign, including the creation of a nationwide educational system. Here, he poses with Thai schoolboys dressed in European clothing.**

The Rise of Nationalism

After ascending the throne in 1910, King Vajiravudh (Rama VI) encouraged a spirit of nationalism among the Thai population. During his fifteen-year reign, he wrote many articles and spoke frequently about the need for loyalty and devotion to the nation. He also organized the highly visible Wild Tiger Corps, a military organization and patriotic civic group.

King Rama VI created the Wild Tiger Corps in 1911 to provide civil servants with military training. The king hoped that the Wild Tiger Corps would help maintain law and order in rural areas and serve as reserve troops during war. A junior division, the Tiger Cubs, was also created.

During World War I (1914–1918), Siam allied itself with France and Great Britain and declared war against Germany. A small force of Thai soldiers went to Europe and joined the fighting. After the war, France and Britain made new treaties with Siam and gave the Thai a more favorable trade arrangement.

In 1932 a group of dissatisfied military and civilian leaders carried out a coup d'état (a swift, forceful change of government) against the monarchy. Many of these leaders were impatient with the lack of democracy under a system of government ruled by one person. The economic difficulties that the country had faced during the worldwide depression of the 1920s and 1930s also spurred the rebels into action.

The leaders of the coup removed the officials appointed by King Prajadhipok (Rama VII), who had taken over the throne in 1925, and reorganized the government. They established a constitution that took away most of the king's power and gave it to elected legislative representatives. This move made Siam a constitutional monarchy—an arrangement that recognized the king as the symbolic ruler but removed his power to administer the country.

Civilian leaders of the coup controlled the government until 1938, when Phibun Songgram, a nationalist leader from the Thai army, became prime minister. Under Phibun's administration, the name of the country was changed from Siam to Thailand in 1939. Phibun's government also pushed for the return of Thai territory that the French and British had absorbed at the turn of the century. After several minor battles against the French in 1940 and 1941, Thailand reclaimed a portion of its lost lands.

World War II and Its Results

During World War II, the Japanese invaded Thailand on December 8, 1941. They fought Thai troops for several hours before Phibun accepted their demand for free access to Burma and Malaya. Later in

Japanese Premier General Tojo reviews a regiment of Thai troops. After Japan invaded Thailand during World War II, the Thai sided with Japan and its allies.

the month, Thailand sided with Japan against the Allies (Britain, France, and the United States, among others).

Many Thai opposed Thailand's official pro-Japanese stand, and they began the Free Thai movement. As the alliance with the Japanese became more like a foreign occupation, Phibun's government became less and less accepted by the Thai. Phibun was forced from office in mid-1944. The governmental ministers who succeeded Phibun came from the country's civilian leaders. The Free Thai movement became more prominent, and as the war drew to a close, members of the anti-Japanese group met openly in Bangkok. When the war ended in 1945, the Thai government rejected its previous alliance with Japan.

After the war, peace agreements forced Thailand to give up the territory it had regained from France. Pridi Phanomyong, who had been a powerful influence among the civilian politicians since the 1930s, became prime minister in 1946. Pridi was popular with the Thai because of his strong anti-Japanese views. His leadership quickly ended, however, when King Ananda Mahidol (Rama VIII) was found dead in his palace. Although reportedly the result of an accidental gunshot wound, the king's death aroused concern about the government's role in royal security. Pridi resigned and left the country.

Ananda's brother, Bhumibol Adulyadej (Rama IX), became king in 1946. (Bhumibol still reigned as monarch in the early twenty-first century.) Because of Pridi's fall from power, civilian politicians lost their approval among the Thai people. In November 1947, Phibun and the military had enough popular support to attempt another coup.

After overthrowing the government, the new regime held elections in early 1948 that confirmed Phibun as leader of the country.

Coups and Constitutions

Phibun's government withstood several attempted coups in the late 1940s and early 1950s. Various political groups urged factions within the military to act against the government, but Phibun's larger group of military supporters was always strong enough to thwart opposition.

Phibun was fiercely anticommunist during his administration. Thailand refused, for example, to recognize the communist regime that founded the People's Republic of China in 1949. Furthermore, new laws restricted and even harassed Chinese residents of Thailand. The Thai government also supported anticommunist movements in Korea and Vietnam.

Some Thai believed Phibun's government was ineffective. As a result, Field Marshal Sarit Thanarat overthrew Phibun in 1957. Sarit suspended the laws of the land—including voting rights—and called for a new constitution. In the absence of an active constitution, Sarit ruled Thailand under martial (military) law.

Sarit, like Phibun, was strongly anticommunist, but he also managed the economy well—something Phibun had not done. Under Sarit's leadership, sanitation improved and more areas of the country received electricity. The field marshal welcomed foreign investment and sponsored new industries, which led to increased employment. In 1963 Sarit died, and his deputy, General Thanom Kittikachorn, succeeded him.

In 1963 **General Thanom Kittikachorn *(second from left)*** became prime minister after the death of Field Marshal Sarit Thanarat.

Thanom gradually restored political rights in Thailand, beginning in 1967 with elections for city posts in Bangkok. In 1968 a new constitution was put into effect, and elections for positions in the nation's legislature were held during the next year. But a weakening economy and the presence of communist forces on Thailand's borders—especially in Laos—prompted Thanom to suspend the constitution in 1971 and to set up another military government.

Thanom introduced a new constitution in 1972, but many university students were not satisfied with the proposed structure of government. In early 1973 the students demonstrated for democratic reforms. The protests grew stronger over the months, until mid-October, when crowds of up to five hundred thousand people gathered in Bangkok. The government troops fired on the assembled protesters and killed some of them. King Bhumibol intervened and negotiated with Thanom. As a result, Thanom and his top officials resigned their posts and left the country.

Another constitution was enacted in 1974, and new elections in 1975 brought in a civilian government. The administration, however, struggled to maintain unity among its own leaders. When Thanom returned to Thailand in 1976, students demonstrated against his presence. Later that year, another coup ousted the civilian government, voided the constitution, and put Thailand under martial law.

Another constitution was drafted in 1978, and Thai administrations continued to revolve in and out of power. In 1980 General Prem Tinsulanonda became prime minister, and his government survived coup attempts in 1981, 1983, and 1985. The king steadily backed Prem, and an increase in the prime minister's supporters in the legislature strengthened his control of the government. Prem also organized a campaign against communist guerrillas operating in Thailand, limiting the influence of communist revolutionaries within Thailand and preventing its communist neighbors from expanding into the nation's territory.

In July 1988, popular elections were held for the national assembly. The newly elected legislative body chose former army general Chatichai Choonhavan to be the new prime minister. Although the transfer of power from Prem to the new leader went smoothly, conflict between the military leadership and civilian government continued. In February 1991, General Sunthorn Kongsompon overthrew Chatichai in a bloodless coup. Sunthorn declared martial law, dissolved the national assembly, and suspended Thailand's constitution. The military chose business executive Anand Panyarachun to lead the nation's interim government as prime

Chatichai Choonhavan *(left)* was just one of many Thai leaders during the 1980s and 1990s to be overthrown in a bloodless coup.

minister. A new constitution that protected the military's interests was proclaimed in December.

Old Issues and New Hope

Thailand's government underwent yet another change in April 1992, when General Suchinda Kraprayoon, head of Thailand's armed forces, declared himself prime minister. Disenchanted with military control of the government, crowds of protesters in Bangkok took to the streets in May 1992 demanding the removal of Suchinda and the establishment of a democratically elected government. Suchinda was forced to resign. In June the king appointed Anand Panyarachun prime minister, and a constitutional amendment guaranteed future prime ministers be elected members of the national assembly.

Anand worked to reduce military authority in state affairs and to curb corruption. He arranged for general elections, which took place in September 1992. The new prime minister, Chuan Leekpai, announced plans to wipe out government corruption and decentralize the government. But by 1993, political parties and the general populace expressed dissatisfaction with the slow progress of his plans. Nonetheless, Chuan was able to introduce a series of constitutional amendments, including voting reforms that changed the eligible voting age to eighteen and that provided voting rights for women. Chuan's approval rating remained low, however, and in 1995, amid a land-reform scandal, he was forced to step down.

Chuan's successor, Banharn Silapa-Archa, fared no better. Banharn was forced to relinquish his post a year later due to allegations of corruption. Chavalit Yongchaiyudh took the reins until late 1997, when Chuan Leekpai was reelected prime minister. A new constitution based on democratic reforms was also introduced in October of that year.

Political instability was not the only problem the government faced. In May 1997, the economy underwent a financial crisis. Regionally, Asian stock markets had grown unstable. Coupled with the burden of political instability and rising debts due to modernization, Thailand's economy suffered when foreign investors pulled out of the country. The country fell into one of the worst recessions it had ever seen. Many business owners lost everything, and unemployment rates soared.

> "Thailand's past and future success is based on its openness to foreigners and its participation in a globalizing world. . . . We realize that our economy is susceptible to powerful external forces—both positive and negative—and that we must be prepared to adapt to such global events."
>
> —Prime Minister Thaksin Shinawatra

Chuan once again lost public favor. In the 2001 elections, business tycoon Thaksin Shinawatra was elected prime minister by a landslide. Within months of taking office, Thaksin's administration created a program to offer cheap health care to poor Thai. In addition, he provided credit to poor villages and farmers. This credit was for villagers who wanted to receive more job training or to develop their own small businesses, which would in turn stimulate the economy. In addition, the government agreed to suspend repayment of loans for three years. The new prime minister has not escaped controversy, however. Shortly after assuming leadership, he was accused of concealing assets and tax evasion. Despite these allegations and a dip in his ratings, Thaksin remains, overall, a popular leader.

Government

Thailand has been a constitutional monarchy, in which the king serves as head of state, since 1932. The king's political power is limited, but he plays an important role as a symbol of national unity. The king gives his approval to governmental appointments presented by the prime minister (the head of government) and

King Bhumibol

the national assembly. He is named the head of the armed forces and the upholder of Buddhism, the country's official religion.

The Thai government adopted a new constitution in 1997, giving the people more political power. The Thai government is a parliamentary system, and the national assembly is the highest governing body. The national assembly consists of the house of representatives and the senate. The house of representatives has five hundred members who are publicly elected and who serve for four years. The senate is made up of two hundred members who are publicly elected and who serve six-year terms. These two branches of the national assembly write and endorse laws.

The prime minister carries out the day-to-day administration of the government. The prime minister must be chosen from the house of representatives and approved by the national assembly. As the head of government, the prime minister is also the leader of the cabinet.

The supreme court is the highest court in Thailand. The nation also has a court of appeals and courts of first instance. Local courts administer laws concerning marriage, inheritance, and other family matters. In the southern region—where many Thai are Malay Muslims (followers of the Islamic religion)—local *qadi* (Islamic judges) administer Sharia (law based on the Quran, Islam's holy book).

Thailand is divided into seventy-six provinces, each of which is ruled by a governor. Groups of villages organize themselves into associations called *tambols.* One person, known as the *kamnan,* is elected from among the village leaders to represent the tambol to the provincial governor and to help solve regional disputes.

THE PEOPLE

Thailand is home to 62.4 million people. Thailand once faced a population explosion that could have further strained an already overcrowded area. In an effort to bring the growth rate under control, the Thai government began promoting family planning as early as the 1970s. Use of contraceptives and smaller families cut the population growth rate from 3.2 percent in the 1960s to less than 1 percent in 2000. At the current rate, Thailand's population will reach about 72 million by 2050.

Thailand is primarily a rural nation, with 70 percent of its population living on farms or in villages. Higher-paying jobs and educational opportunities have led to an influx into the cities, however, and especially into Bangkok. While many people returned to the countryside after the economy crashed in the 1990s, the country's major cities still face limited housing, traffic congestion, and other issues related to overcrowding.

Most city dwellers live in apartment buildings with stores or businesses on the first floor. Young married couples frequently live in their own apartments, and usually husbands and wives both work. If a

couple has children, it is not uncommon for both parents to work out-side the home. Adults in the city work in a wide variety of sectors, from retail to high-tech industries. On weekends many families leave the city to visit relatives in the countryside.

Rural families live differently from their urban counterparts. Most people living in the countryside farm or run small businesses. Many gen-erations often live under the same roof, and adults in a village help care for all the children, whether or not they are related. Village families typi-cally live in wood homes, often built on stilts to protect them from floods.

▶ Ethnic Groups

All citizens of Thailand, no matter what their ethnic ties, are called Thai. But a group known as ethnic Thai make up 84 percent of Thailand's population. The ethnic Thai fall into several subgroups that are determined by geographic location within the country and by distinctive language variations.

Chinese settlers have been an important part of Thailand's ethnic composition since the 1800s and currently make up 12 percent of the population. After World War II, the Thai government passed laws that limited the number of Chinese immigrants. From the 1950s through the 1970s, the Chinese language was restricted for fear of the spread of communism. Because of this, many descendants of these Chinese settlers grew up speaking Thai and consider Thailand their native country. Intermarriage with ethnic Thai is common, which led to the rapid integration of many Chinese into Thai communities. Late in the twentieth century, however, many ethnic Chinese workers began competing with Thai laborers for jobs. This situation, coupled with the deep antagonism that many Thai felt toward the People's Republic of China and its communist system, has prompted anti-Chinese sentiments among some Thai.

Immigrants from China, like this woman living in the Khorat Plateau, form Thailand's largest minority population.

These **Malay children** are dressed in traditional Muslim attire. Most Malay are followers of Islam.

About 3 percent of Thailand's population is made up of Malays who live in the southern peninsular region, near the Malaysian border. Almost all Malay Thai are members of Islam—a religion founded in Saudi Arabia during the seventh century A.D. Malay Thai predominantly work as rubber tree planters, farmers, and fishers.

Northern and western Thailand have small ethnic groups known as hill peoples. One of the largest of these groups is the Hmong. This

Hmong woman

group migrated into Thailand from Laos and China at the beginning of the nineteenth century. They live in mountain villages and raise rice, maize (corn), and opium poppies. Because poppies are the source of opium, an illegal drug, Thai authorities have destroyed many poppy harvests and encourage the Hmong and other poppy growers to raise other crops.

Warfare and lack of economic opportunity have brought thousands of refugees to Thailand in recent years. By the end of 2001, the refugee population—mostly from Burma, Laos, and Vietnam—numbered almost three hundred thousand. The Thai government is working to quickly resettle or repatriate the refugees.

Language

The Thai language belongs to the Thai family of languages. Thai speech consists mostly of one-syllable words, each of which has several translations. Thai speech depends on the tone of the spoken word to distinguish one meaning from another. The five tones—rising or falling, high or low, or an even tone—indicate different meanings for a single word. The position in which the word appears in a sentence also helps to determine its meaning.

The Thai writing system has forty-four consonants and thirty-two vowels, with tone markings placed above the letters. The script that King Rama Khamhaeng developed in the fourteenth century was based on a pattern of Khmer characters. Thai letters are curved and flowing, and they are written left to right without punctuation.

The four dialects of the Thai language correspond to the country's four main geographical regions: central, northern, northeastern (Khorat Plateau), and southern. Vocabulary is basically the same for all of the dialects, but the tonal patterns are different. After becoming familiar with tones of another region, speakers of different dialects can communicate with each other.

Central Thai is the official language of the nation, and it is used in schools, in newspapers, and in television and radio broadcasts. Malay Thai, many of whom are not fluent in Thai, speak the Malay language. Most Chinese Thai speak the official language as well as Chinese. Members of the various hill groups speak one of several non-Thai languages and usually know only enough Thai to function as traders.

The ornate curves of written Thai are showcased in these billboards.

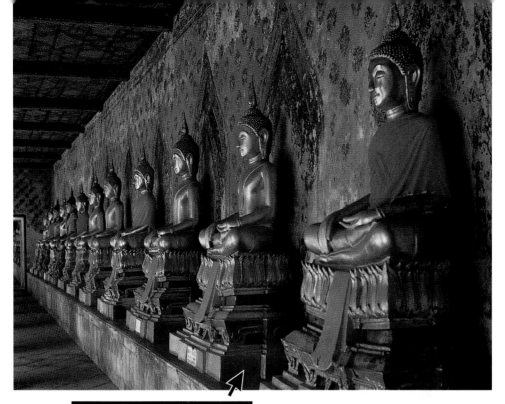

This **row of golden Buddha statues** is enshrined at Wat Po in Bangkok. Buddhists often drape Buddha figures with orange monastic robes.

◉ Religion

Ninety-five percent of the people in Thailand practice Buddhism. Buddhists follow the teachings of Siddhartha Gautama, the Buddha (Buddha means "Enlightened One"), who founded Buddhism in India in the sixth century B.C.

Buddha's teachings include belief in a constant cycle of death and rebirth called reincarnation. He also believed that freedom from suffering could be achieved through detachment from material things. Buddhism teaches tolerance toward all and belief in the idea of karma, in which every act has a consequence.

Buddhism in Thailand has its roots in a Buddhist sect named Theravada, meaning "Way of the Elders," which Sri Lankan monks introduced to the region. This branch of Buddhism focuses particularly on the monastic way of life and on the Buddhist scriptures known as the Tripitika.

It is customary for young Thai men over the age of twenty to become monks for a period of time—from a few days to several months. As monks, they receive offerings of food, study Buddhist writings, and pray each day.

Many Chinese Thai follow Confucianism, which is a philosophical approach to life that

Buddhist monk

THE ROLE OF WOMEN

Thai women historically have had considerable influence in Thai society. In rural areas, property is usually passed down from mothers to daughters, and women frequently run the family farm. It is not uncommon for women to control the family finances. Education and career opportunities are widely available to women, although women are less likely to receive higher education.

Yet in politics, women do not have acceptance and equality. By 2001 only 10 percent of government workers were female. Higher posts, such as cabinet positions, are even less open to women, with only 6 percent of these offices filled by female officials.

stresses the development of moral character. Begun in the sixth century B.C. by a Chinese scholar named Confucius, this system of thought emphasizes order in family and civic life, as well as respect for one's ancestors.

The Malay Thai are predominantly Muslims—followers of Islam. Muslims believe in Allah and the prophet Muhammad, pray five times per day, give alms (charity) to the poor, fast during the holy month of Ramadan, and, if possible, make a pilgrimage to the holy city of Mecca in Saudi Arabia on at least one occasion in their lifetime.

The ethnic groups living in the mountains—as well as many people who otherwise follow Buddhism, Confucianism, and Islam—practice a number of local religious beliefs. They ask spirits for aid and protection by offering them incense, flowers, and food. They leave these items in miniature houses built for the spirits. Small numbers of people, mainly in Bangkok, practice Christianity or Hinduism.

◉ Education

Early Thai education consisted of either basic training for boys joining a monastery or special tutors for children of the royal household and noble families. The majority of Thailand's population—village farmers—saw little use for literacy. It wasn't until the late nineteenth century that King Rama V recognized the importance of an educated people and began to make changes to the educational system. In 1898 the Education Proclamation made instruction more accessible to the general populace.

In the early twentieth century, Thai leaders began to plan a new educational system. In 1921 the king decreed a policy of free education for all Thai children. The first formal education plan was introduced in 1932, and it called for four years of elementary school and eight years of secondary school. In the 1940s and 1950s, the government built public schools and trained teachers to help educate the nation's children on a large scale. By the 1990s, the government focused on availability and quality of secondary and higher education. Special programs worked to improve the quality of science, mathematics, and foreign language instruction, and more secondary schools were launched. The government continues to make education a priority for the Thai people.

Attendance at primary school is compulsory for all Thai children between the ages of six and eleven. Through a combination of public and private schools, 87 percent of the eligible population is enrolled at the primary level. About 56 percent go on to the secondary stage, which lasts from ages twelve to eighteen. Thailand's literacy rate of 96 percent for men and 92 percent for women is above average for Southeast Asian countries.

Of Thailand's twenty state universities and twenty-six private colleges and universities, twelve are located in Bangkok—including Chulalongkorn University, founded in 1917, and Thammasat University, opened in 1934. The government has established several universities in locations other than Bangkok to make higher education more widely available. For example, Chiang Mai University opened in

Students study in a classroom in a secondary school in the village of Lahu.

1964 in the northern Thai city from which it takes its name. Thailand also has several vocational and agricultural institutions.

> To find out more about the various customs of people in Thailand (including ethnic Thai, Chinese, Malay, and Hmong), to learn some basic Thai words, and to get the most up-to-date population figures, visit vgsbooks.com.

Health

Health care in Thailand steadily improved during the second half of the twentieth century. About half of the population has organized health insurance, and widespread vaccination initiatives have reduced the occurrence of cholera, tetanus, tuberculosis, and smallpox. Chemical sprays have reduced the malaria-carrying mosquito population, and drugs to treat the disease are widely used. The government has improved sanitation facilities and has increased the availability of safe drinking water. As a result, intestinal diseases, which can be fatal, occur less frequently.

In 1974 the government's Public Welfare Department set up family-planning centers in every region of the nation. These centers not only

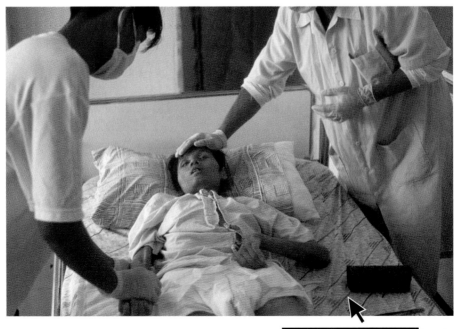

Although great strides have been made, the **Thai health care system** is still overwhelmed by the demand for treatment.

provide education about family planning but also inform the public about nutrition, sanitation, and disease prevention.

The government continues to push for better health care. By the beginning of the twenty-first century, Thailand had more than 1,300 hospitals, 16,500 physicians, and 988,000 nurses working throughout the country. High-quality health care is available to those who live outside Bangkok, previously the nation's only medical center.

Etiquette is taken very seriously in Thailand. People greet each other with a *wai*, a gesture of palms joined together and placed between the chest and forehead. In addition, feet should never openly point to someone, and a person's head should never be touched by strangers. Both are considered disrespectful.

These and other measures have helped increase Thai life expectancy to 72 years. The infant mortality rate, the number of infants who die after a live birth, has also improved because of better health care. In 2002 the infant mortality rate was 22 out of every 1,000 live births.

But the Thai still face serious health problems. Because of its position in the Golden Triangle—the drug-producing region located at the borders of Laos, Burma, and Thailand—illegal drugs are widely available in Thailand. Despite the government's antidrug programs and strict drug laws, heroin addiction rates continue to rise. And widespread methamphetamine abuse among young people has forced many Thai schools to conduct random drug tests on students.

One of the most serious health problems in Bangkok and in the country's other tourist centers is related to drug use and prostitution. An estimated one hundred thousand Thai in Bangkok accept money in exchange for sexual encounters, a practice that increases the threat of contracting human immunodeficiency virus (HIV) and acquired immunodeficiency syndrome (AIDS). During the early and mid-1990s, the Thai government spent $80 million a year on HIV/AIDS education. The program reduced the number of reported cases from 400,000 in 1986 to 50,000 in 1995. But since 1996, the government has decreased its HIV/AIDS-awareness expenditures, and, as a result, HIV/AIDS infections have begun to increase. In 2002 Thailand announced an HIV vaccine trial, the world's largest to date, which will attempt to determine the effectiveness of an HIV vaccine.

CULTURAL LIFE

Thailand has a rich cultural life that dates back to its earliest settlers. Through the centuries, outside influences from India, China, and Europe have impacted Thai artists, who have adapted foreign forms of expression in a way that made them unique to Thailand.

Two important elements helped shape the art of Thailand—the monarchy and religion. The Thai rulers supported the arts throughout the centuries, often dictating styles and even contributing to the arts as writers and musicians.

Religion also played a driving force in Thailand's cultural life. Most early major artistic works of architecture, painting, and music were inspired by Buddhist themes. This religious influence is seen in the many temples and Buddhist images found throughout the country.

Holidays and Festivals

Thailand celebrates many holidays and festivals, many of which are linked to Buddhist rituals. One of the most important festivals is

Songkran (Thai New Year) in April. Songkran, a three-day water festival, takes place at Thailand's hottest time of the year. People have fun by splashing water on one another. Parades and dances make up a big part of the celebration too. People also wash things thoroughly to clean away the old and make way for the new. Sprinkling water over the hands of monks and elders is also part of the festival and is done to show respect.

Loi Krathong, the Candle Festival, takes place in the fall, usually late October or November, under a full moon. Candles are placed inside special cups known as krathong or on small bamboo boats that float down the rivers and canals. The Thai believe that this carries away bad deeds. Fireworks, candle-decorating competitions, and local fairs are also be held during Loi Krathong.

Local and regional fairs occur throughout the year in various parts of the country. The Royal Ploughing Ceremony takes place in Bangkok in May. During this ceremony, the Thai celebrate the beginning of the

A wild and raucous water festival, Songkran (Thai New Year) is celebrated in April. Here, celebrants in Chiang Mai douse each other with hoses.

rice growing season. Phuket, which has a large Chinese population, holds a Vegetarian Festival during September and October. For ten days, people eat no meat as a way of honoring their Chinese ancestors. Parades and ceremonies also pay tribute to the Chinese immigrants who moved to the area in the nineteenth century.

In addition to these festivals, Thailand celebrates several national and Buddhist holidays. The King's Birthday and the Queen's Birthday are both national holidays. On these holidays, towns are bedecked with colored lights and other decorations. Families celebrate with large meals, preparing both traditional dishes and family favorites.

Food

Thai food is often spicy with contrasting sweet, sour, and salty tastes. From the Chinese, Thai cooks learned how to prepare small, cut-up pieces of food by stirring them in a very hot, lightly oiled pan—a technique known as stir-frying. Thai cuisine also uses curry, a combination of spices that originated in India. Coconut milk sometimes flavors Thai food and mellows the spicier dishes.

The Thai eat rice with almost every meal. People in the Khorat Plateau prefer the short-grained, sticky variety of rice that grows in the area. But most of the people of Thailand eat the more common long-grained rice.

Seafood from the Gulf of Thailand and fish from the nation's rivers are an important part of the Thai diet. Mussels, crabs, lobsters, scallops, shrimp, and squid are often served at meals. The many varieties of fish are eaten in fresh, salted, dried, and pickled forms.

Bananas, pineapples, papayas, and mangoes are among the most popular fruits in Thailand. Rambutans (red, oval-shaped fruit), mangosteens (reddish brown fruit with a flavor similar to a mixture of peach and pineapple), and shaddocks (an Asian version of grapefruit) are native to the region.

Noodles made from rice, eggs, or mung beans are a regular part of Thai meals. Fried rice, curried chicken, and salads made with vegetables and small amounts of beef are some favorite dishes. At most of their meals, the Thai use a sauce called *nam pla prig,* which is made from fish sauce, garlic, red peppers, and lemon juice.

MANGO AND STICKY RICE

Mangoes are a Thai favorite and are served in many ways. This sweet dish is a popular dessert at home and in the marketplaces.

2 c. glutinous rice (found in Asian supermarkets)

1¼ c. canned coconut milk

pinch of salt

2 tbsp. sugar

1¼ c. water

2 large, ripe mangoes

1. Soak rice in cold water for at least one hour. Drain.
2. In saucepan, bring rice, coconut milk, salt, sugar, and water to a boil. Stir and reduce heat. Simmer uncovered for 8 to 10 minutes, or until all liquid is absorbed. Remove from heat. Cover and let stand 5 minutes.
3. Transfer rice to a steamer or double boiler. Steam over boiling water for 15–20 minutes, or until rice is cooked through.
4. Mold rice into small cups lined with plastic wrap. Cool to room temperature.
5. Peel and slice mangoes. Unmold rice onto plate. Top with mango. Serves 4.

Full of fragrant dishes and strong spices, Thai cuisine is varied and colorful. Bangkok's open-air markets provide the perfect place to sample local flavors.

Meals in Thailand are often artistically arranged, especially during national festivals such as the King's Birthday or New Year's Day. During traditional celebrations, the low tables in Thai dining areas are arrayed with fruits and vegetables cut into decorative shapes. Diners commonly sit on the floor, serve themselves from small bowls arranged around their plates, and eat with forks and spoons.

◉ Literature

Because education was reserved for monks and nobles, most Thai relied on storytellers to pass on tales. As the country's monarchs began to see the importance of an educated populace, the written word became increasingly important. The first work recognized as Thai literature is an inscription written in 1292 by King Rama Khamhaeng and is known as "Inscription No. 1." The inscription describes the kingdom of Sukhothai, as well as the lifestyle of its people. Rama Khamhaeng is credited with developing the Thai writing system and is often called the father of Thai literature.

The themes of traditional Thai writing became more religious as Buddhist influence grew. By the Ayutthayan dynasty, Thai literature was flourishing. One of the most important early Ayutthayan works is the *Three Worlds of Phraruang.* Written in the fourteenth century, this work offers insight into three realms: heaven, earth, and hell. Scholars believe that the piece was written by King Li Thai. Poetry also thrived at this time, reaching its golden age in the mid-seventeenth century under King Narai. Long poems, which usually describe a journey, offer historians a better understanding of life during this period.

Fiction first emerged in Thailand during the Rattanakosin period, founded in 1782, when Chao Phraya Phra Khlang penned a historical romance. Sunthorn Phu, considered the most important Thai poet, also lived during this time. His masterpiece, *Phra Aphaimani,* is a romantic epic that tells the story of a prince who falls in love with a mermaid.

Historically, Thai stories were most often told in verse, but modern Thai literature has largely abandoned poetic form. Thai writers in the twenty-first century express themselves in novels, short stories, and essays, sometimes writing in English. Important novels of the early twentieth century include Prince Arkartdamkeung Rapheephat's *The Circus of Life* and Dokmai Sot's *The Good Person.* Both deal with the conflict between Thai and Western cultures. Contemporary twenty-first century writers include Pira Sudham, who writes about country life in the northeastern region, and Sanitsuda Ekachai, whose works examine the pressures and dreams of everyday Thai.

THE *RAMAKIEN*

Around the fifth century B.C., an Indian poet named Valmiki composed an epic called the *Ramayana.* The Thai version of this tale, called the *Ramakien*, probably originated around the second century A.D. While it is a sacred story among Hindus, Thai writers have removed religious elements from the story and added characters and variations to make it a uniquely Thai tale. Though many Thai poets and writers have created versions of this classic, the most famous is probably Rama I's, composed in 1807.

The plot of the *Ramakien* revolves around a Thai prince named Rama. Prince Rama renounces his throne and runs away with his wife, Sita. But the demon king, Tosakanth, abducts Sita. Rama must gather support from an army of monkeys to win her back. Several subplots original to the Thai version incorporate Thai history and mythology into the story.

Dance and Theater

Dance and drama are highly developed arts in Thailand. Folk epics—especially the *Ramayana*, an Indian tale of the god Rama, called the *Ramakien* in Thai—are enacted by dancers with precise and graceful movements. *Khon* is the most formal style of dance. Performers wear masks and elaborate costumes decorated with costume jewelry. The movements of the dancers express parts of the story. Khon dancers do

not speak but are accompanied by a chorus that communicates the necessary dialogue.

Lakhon is a less formal style of Thai dance. Lakhon performers do not wear masks, and they speak the lines of the story. Dancers use expressive hand gestures and stylized movements to portray specific emotions. Many Thai consider lakhon to be the most graceful of the nation's dance forms, and female dancers most often perform the movements.

Thai shadow plays, known as *nang,* are enacted by artists who use the cutout shapes of characters to tell a story. By moving the shapes in front of a lamp, nang players cast shadows onto a large screen for the audience to see. *Hun* is Thai puppet theater, and the puppets are worked by players who sit below a specially built stage. Musicians typically accompany Khon, lakhon, nang, hun, and other forms of dance and theater.

Music

Thai music is a combination of elements from different cultures, most notably Chinese, Indian, and Khmer. While the instruments and melodies are derived from other traditions, Thai musicians have developed a very distinct form. Traditional Thai instruments include the *jakhae* (guitar), *khwang* (gong), *khaen* (bamboo pipes), and a variety of *glawng* (drums).

Traditional Thai music is unwritten but has survived because each generation of musicians has passed it on to the next. In the 1930s and

1940s, however, Thailand's traditional music began to die out. The music was considered unmodern, and young musicians no longer wanted to learn how to play the instruments or the melodies. Modern Thai musicians such as Montree Tramote and Khunying Phaitoon Kittivan work to save traditional Thai music from extinction. By devising a system to write the music in Western notation, performers hope to preserve this unique art form for future generations of musicians.

Western music, particularly classical music and jazz, has also had an impact on Thai musicians. In 1982 musicians formed the Bangkok Symphony Orchestra. Jazz clubs have also grown in popularity. King Bhumibol himself is considered a talented jazz musician. Western pop music, which was introduced to the country during the 1950s, remains a popular genre.

Arts and Crafts

For centuries painting and sculpture in Thailand depicted religious imagery and stories. Painters were confined to representing religious and royal themes or to creating illustrations for books. Sculpture was limited to stylized images of Buddha and the Hindu gods. Not until Italian artist Corado Feroci moved to Thailand in 1924 did these art forms undergo a massive transformation. Feroci, who eventually became a Thai citizen and changed his name to Silpa Bhirasri, is credited with establishing modern art in Thailand. Contemporary artists include painters such as Thawan Dachanee and sculptors such as Misiem Yipintsoi.

Silversmith

Crafts have long been an important part of Thailand's culture. Thailand's tradition of handicrafts is widely varied. Thai silversmiths are world famous for their elegant silver bowls, boxes, and trays. Smiths cut or shape sheets of silver into intricate designs. Some artisans engrave silver and then rub lead or copper over it to create a raised pattern.

Probably the most famous Thai handicraft is silk making. Thailand's weavers are internationally famous for their silk. The Khorat Plateau is the center of the silk industry, where each worker daily weaves 2 to 3 yards (1.8 to 2.7 m) of silk cloth on handlooms. Women in northeast Thailand produce rich, glossy fabrics in patterns and in solid colors. Thai silk is sold worldwide.

The production of lacquerware is another widespread Thai handicraft. Lacquerware artisans brush layers of lacquer, or varnish, onto wood and polish each layer with charcoal. The piece is then engraved with a sharp instrument and soaked in red dye. The engraved part absorbs the dye, but the polished areas remain black. Other important crafts include pottery, wood carvings, and colorful hand-painted umbrellas. These products are sold locally and to tourists as souvenirs.

Architecture

Ancient temples and centuries-old palaces stand next to modern sky-scrapers in Thai cities. While secular buildings have always been impor-tant, the most revered type of architecture in Thailand is the *wat* (temple).

Little is known about Thai architecture before the Sukhothai Empire. The earliest Thai buildings were made of wood, which rots quickly in the humid climate of Southeast Asia. Two exceptions are Wat Phra Boromthat and Wat Phra Kaeo. These structures, both located in the southern region of the country, date back more than 1,200 years.

The Sukhothai period of the thirteenth and fourteenth cen-turies is marked by major advancements in architecture. Influences from the Khmer in Cambodia are seen in the use of sandstone and brick as well as the unique conical shape of wat tow-ers. Important examples from this period include Wat Chang Lom and Wat Mahathat.

During this time, Thai builders developed the elements that became unique to Thai wats. The *chedi*, a dome-shaped structure that housed the relics of holy men and kings, is the most sacred and elabo-rate feature. The *bot*, the second most important element, is an assembly hall where monks medi-tate and ceremonies are performed. The bot contains the wat's main image of the Buddha.

Other elements introduced dur-ing the Sukhothai period include

SPIRIT HOUSES

Early Thai practiced animism, a religious system based on the belief that all objects have a spirit. Most modern homes and public buildings have a spirit house—a miniature house where spirits reside. The Thai believe that the houses keep the spirits happy and out of mischief.

Wat Mahathat was built around 1374, during the reign of King Rama I. The temple complex houses Mahachulalongkorn Buddhist University, one of the two highest seats of Buddhist learning in Thailand.

the *prang* (spires) and the *wihan* (a smaller assembly hall). *Chofa,* a roof decoration that looks like animal horns, is probably the most recognizable wat element.

The Ayutthayan (sixteenth to eighteenth centuries) and Bangkok (from 1782 to present) periods adopted the Sukhothai style, though materials and design techniques were refined. Important structures from these periods include the Wat Watthanaam and Wat Chumphon, built in the Ayutthayan style, and Wat Phra Kaeo and the secular Grand Palace, both done in the Bangkok style.

Once Thailand opened its doors to Europe, Western elements began to creep into the country's architecture. For contemporary Thai architects, anything goes, and cities boast a hodgepodge of styles—from native Thai elements to Western modernism.

Sports and Recreation

People in several Southeast Asian countries engage in the sport of kite-flying. Stretched tightly on bamboo frames, kites in Thailand are made of beautifully illustrated paper. Teams fly large kites in aerial fights, and each kite tries to make the others fall to the ground.

Takraw is another sport played throughout much of Southeast Asia. Players hit a ball woven from tough palm stems (rattan) back and forth over a net or into a hoop. Players keep the ball in the air by bouncing it off their heads or feet, but they may not use their hands. A team scores points when it puts the ball through the hoop or when the other team allows the ball to hit the ground.

Muay Thai, or kickboxing, is one of Thailand's most popular sports. Boxers use their bare feet, elbows, knees, and gloved hands as they fight each other. A traditional ceremony in which contestants honor their teachers through prayer precedes each match. Musicians playing traditional Thai instruments accompany this prayer and continue playing throughout the match.

THE ECONOMY

For most of its history, Thailand's economy was rooted in agriculture, especially the cultivation of rice. As Southeast Asian economies began to industrialize during the early and mid-twentieth century, small businesses and factories sprang up in Thailand. Thai exports began to include nonfarming commodities such as textiles.

By the late 1980s and early 1990s, foreign investment allowed Thailand's manufacturing sector to surpass agriculture as the chief producer of exports. The economy boomed, averaging almost 9 percent annual growth between 1985 and 1995, the world's highest growth rate at the time. Financial experts predicted that the country would earn a place among the world's economic leaders early in the new millennium.

But in 1997, financial crisis turned Thailand's boom into a bust. The Thai government had allowed its banks to borrow money from foreign countries to lend both locally and abroad. Many of these loans went to sectors of low productivity, however. And the country was importing more than it was exporting. As labor costs increased and

production decreased, Thai products became more expensive. Important Thai exports lost their competitive edge in the world market. Many local businesses failed, and unemployment soared.

Foreign investors pulled out of the Thai economy. They exchanged their baht for dollars, leaving a huge supply of baht with little international demand for it. The Thai government dipped into the country's reserve of foreign currency, causing these reserves to dry up. This left Thailand with huge foreign debts and a diminished industrial sector.

In 1998 the government launched several economic recovery programs. In addition, the International Monetary Fund (IMF) offered emergency loans, but not without conditions. The IMF demanded sweeping economic reforms to make the financial process less secretive and, therefore, more transparent to foreign investors.

Thailand's economy began to recover slowly in 1999. The baht stabilized, and the Thai senate passed new legislation to privatize some state-owned businesses. In addition, new bankruptcy and foreclosure laws were passed. For the first time, many Thai banks became open to majority foreign ownership.

The new millennium brought new hope to Thailand as the economy grew by more than 4 percent in 2000 and by about 2 percent in 2001. Inflation rates have dropped, and economic restructuring continues. But the Thai economy is far from full recovery. Rising unemployment rates and a slowdown in the global economy threaten the nation's volatile economy.

Agriculture

Farming makes up 11 percent of Thailand's gross domestic product (GDP), and about half of the country's workforce earns a living in this sector. Thailand's central plain is known as the rice bowl area, because farmers in this region grow most of the rice that is exported. The Chao Phraya River and its tributaries overflow during the southwest monsoon season. Floodwaters cover the paddies (rice fields), which are divided by earthen barriers. Water buffalo are used to plow the flooded fields, and in July workers transplant seedlings from nursery beds into the paddies.

Khlongs help control floodwaters on the central plain. When the rains diminish, the canals carry water from reservoirs formed by dams on the Chao Phraya. In November the winds of the northeast monsoon dry out the paddies, and the farmers harvest the rice. Thailand remains the world's largest exporter of rice.

The Khorat Plateau is less fertile than the rest of the country, but rice can be planted in paddies that are situated near rivers. The farmers in this region grow a short-grained type of rice.

Thailand is the world's largest exporter of rice. **The rice harvest** has remained the most important event in rural Thailand for centuries.

Cassava (a starchy root) has also become one of the region's export crops.

Maize and sugarcane are major crops grown on the edges of the central plain. Situated at a slightly higher elevation, these areas are not likely to flood during the rainy season.

On the southern peninsula, farmers cultivate rice, pineapples, bananas, and cotton. Thai farmers also raise flowers, especially orchids, for local and export markets. Livestock on Thai farms include water buffalo and cattle, both of which are used as draft (load-pulling) animals. Farmers raise pigs, chickens, and ducks as well, mostly for food.

Orchid farm

In some areas of the country, hill people grow opium poppies as a cash (money-earning) crop. The territory on the borders of Myanmar, Laos, and Thailand—where poppies are widely cultivated—is known as the Golden Triangle. While the Thai government continues efforts to stop this illegal activity, about 6 tons (5 metric tons) of opium were produced from local poppy crops during the first few years of the twenty-first century.

Forestry and Fishing

Thailand's forests, which covered about half the land in the mid-1960s, have shrunk to only about 22 percent. Historically, teak has been Thailand's most valuable timber. Because the wood from these trees is strong, durable, and water-resistant, teak was used mostly for furniture and shipbuilding. Evergreen and deciduous (leaf-shedding) trees also provided the raw material for furniture, housing, shipbuilding, and carved artworks. Other profitable trees included mahogany, ebony, rosewood, and rattan palm.

Large-scale logging—to create farmland and to supply wood for fuel and for building material—has left Thailand with very little forest cover of commercial value. In 1989, as a result of this environmental damage, the Thai government imposed a complete ban on commercial logging. This has been difficult to enforce, however. To renew this natural resource, Thailand sponsors a limited reforestation program, replanting mostly fast-growing pine and eucalyptus trees.

Farmers in the southern peninsula grow rubber trees on small plots of land. The sap from the trees—called latex—is the raw material for making rubber. In the 1990s, the quality of latex had greatly improved, leading to a rise in Thailand's production of rubber goods. By the turn of the century, Thailand had become a world leader in the production of natural rubber.

A group of men use the **dragnet fishing method** near Chiang Mai. Many technological advancements have been made in the fishing industry, but some fishers still use older methods.

Fish and other seafood are an important part of Thailand's economy. By the late 1990s, Thailand's total catch had risen to almost 3 million tons (2.7 million metric tons). Sea fishing provides 93 percent of all fish caught by Thai fishers. Improvements such as modernized boats, as well as agreements with some neighboring countries to fish their waters, have helped Thailand develop its fishing industry. Thailand has become the leading exporter of fishery commodities in the world. The shrimp catch has been particularly large, and fresh and frozen shrimp have become a leading Thai export.

Freshwater species are abundant in Thailand's rivers, lakes, khlongs, ponds, and rice paddies. Many rural Thai angle in these waterways, and local markets stock a wide variety of freshwater fish.

Industry and Mining

Industry, which includes mining and manufacturing, accounts for 39 percent of Thailand's GDP. Many of Thailand's industries are located in and around Bangkok—the nation's major import and export center. To combat overcrowding in the country's cities, Thailand is working on a program of rural industrialization. Industries and factories have been relocated to rural areas, offering employment to people in the country and slowing the influx of workers to the cities. Companies from Japan, the United States, and other nations have invested in Thailand's industrial economy. The country's new manufacturing sector produces electronic and electrical goods for local use and for export.

The textile industry has been an important part of Thailand's economy since the early twentieth century. Silk and cotton are woven in many urban mills. Villagers also produce cloth as a way to earn money while working at home. By the late 1990s, textiles contributed 6 percent of the nation's export earnings.

Thai manufacturers have developed a large food-processing industry, and the nation has become one of the world's largest producers of canned tuna. Thailand also puts out a significant portion of the world supply of canned pineapple. Other areas of industrial growth include cement plants and sugarcane refineries.

Thai miners in the southern peninsula dig for tin ore, and Thailand is consistently among the world's top three suppliers of tin. In addition, the nation mines lignite, gypsum, zinc, and iron ore. Precious gemstones, especially diamonds, are another important product of the country's mining sector.

One of Thailand's economic difficulties has been its reliance on petroleum imports, but discoveries of natural gas and oil in the Gulf of Thailand have partly eased this problem. The country has four oil refineries to produce petroleum products for local use, reducing its dependence on oil imports. And in 1999, Thailand's energy sector, which had been state run, began a process of restructuring to make the energy industry more efficient and to reduce the government's investment burden.

THAI SILK

Silk-making is a long and involved process. Weavers must raise their own silkworms. Because the worms eat mulberry leaves, weavers must also grow and tend mulberry trees. Once the silkworms spin a silk cocoon around themselves, the weavers have just ten days before the worm transforms into a moth and destroys its silk cocoon. The weavers drop the cocoons into boiling water, killing the worm, and then unroll the silk. After they have the silk strands, weavers spin and dye the threads. These can then be woven into bolts of cloth.

Go to vgsbooks.com for up-to-date information about Thailand's economy and to use a converter where you can learn how many Thai baht are in one U.S. dollar.

Transportation

The transportation network in Thailand consists of roads, railways, waterways, and domestic and international air routes. More than 97 percent of Thailand's 40,140 miles (64,600 km) of roadway is paved. Buses and cars crisscross the country, and in the cities, rickshas (two-wheeled vehicles pulled by one person), three-wheeled motorized carts, and motorcycles also provide transportation. Because of the population influx into Bangkok, traffic is congested and slow-moving.

The State Railway of Thailand oversees 2,873 miles (4,623 km) of railroad track. Four main routes radiate from Bangkok to the four main geographical districts. The rail lines run to Chiang Mai in the north, to Aranyaprathet in the east, to Ubon Ratchathani on the Khorat Plateau, and to the Malaysian border in the south.

The rivers and khlongs of the central plain provide an extensive transportation route for people and agricultural goods on the way to and from Bangkok. As Thailand's central city, Bangkok is also a crowded port that receives goods from abroad and exports Thai materials and finished products overseas.

Thai Airways International and other airlines fly from Thailand's five international airports, which are located in Bangkok, Chiang Mai, Phuket, Chiang Rai, and Hat Yai. Bangkok Airways is the nation's domestic airline and connects smaller towns to one another and to Bangkok.

GETTING AROUND

The people of Thailand use several modes of transportation. In addition to trains, buses, and autos, there are a variety of unique vehicles. *Saamlors* are three-wheeled bikes, either pedaled or motorized, found in almost every town. *Tuk-tuks*, gas-powered scooters, zip through busy city streets. *Songthaew*, pickups outfitted with benches, serve specific routes or may be hired like taxicabs. Bicycles and motorbikes are also popular in both the cities and the countryside. Long-tailed boats called *hang-yaaws* travel up and down the khlongs of Bangkok.

A Bangkok tuk-tuk makes its way through traffic.

Tourists from all over the world are drawn to the historic and natural wonders of Thailand.

Tourism

Millions of tourists from all over the world come to visit the nation's resorts, beaches, and palaces. Pattaya, southwest of Bangkok, and Phuket are two of the largest resort areas. The ruins of palaces and temples at Ayutthaya and Sukhothai in central Thailand are also popular sites. Tourism slowed in the early 1990s, partly as a result of political instability. Another factor in the downturn was negative publicity focusing on pollution, on the drug trade, on prostitution, and on the spread of AIDS in Thailand. Yet tourism remains an important part of the Thai economy.

With its historical landmarks and varied cultural events, Bangkok attracts the largest number of tourists. One of the most popular tourist stops is the Grand Palace, which is in the oldest part of Bangkok. In the late eighteenth century, King Chakri built the first royal residence on the site. Since then, several kings have constructed their own residences, as well as adding religious and civic buildings. The palace grounds also contain several wats.

The Future

Political instability and economic woes have left Thailand with an uncertain future. An underdeveloped infrastructure and slow reforms have limited the country's economic recovery, and uncontrolled industrial development has led to serious environmental problems such as deforestation and pollution.

Social ills also plague the Thai people. Widespread drug use and diseases such as HIV and AIDS are taking a toll on the nation's young people. In addition, the gap between rich and poor people continues to widen as a small minority get richer and the vast majority get poorer.

Despite these difficulties, the Thai people remain optimistic. A well-educated and hardworking labor force, a history of economic growth, and a strong sense of cultural identity all indicate a promising future for the Land of Smiles.

38,000 B.C.	Nomads live in Southeast Asia.
7000 B.C.	People settle and farm the Ban Chiang and Ban Kao areas.
A.D. 357	Funan has established trading ties with China and India.
900	Khmer Empire expands into what will later become central and northeast Thailand.
1200s	Sri Lankan monks bring Theravada Buddhism to the area.
1238	Thai-speaking immigrants defeat the Khmer and set up a capital in the city of Sukhothai.
1292	King Rama Khamhaeng writes "Inscription No. 1."
1296	Chiang Mai is founded.
1350	Rama Thibodi establishes a new dynasty, centered at Ayutthaya.
1431	Thai soldiers capture and destroy the Khmer capital at Angkor.
1448	King Trailok begins his forty-year reign and reforms the kingdom's administration.
1511	Portuguese traders establish contact with the Thai.
1569	Burmese forces capture Ayutthaya.
1593	Thai king Naresuan defeats Burma's prince in a battle at Nong Sarai.
1608	A Thai ambassador is sent to the Netherlands.
1760	Burmese forces begin a campaign to capture Ayutthaya.
1767	Ayutthaya falls to Burmese forces. Phraya Taksin defeats Burmese troops.
1782	The Chakri dynasty is established. King Rama I builds Wat Phra Kaeo in Bangkok.
1807	King Rama I composes his version of the *Ramayana*.
1826	The Thai kingdom and Great Britain sign the Burney Treaty.
1836	American missionaries open Thailand's first printing house.
1851	Mongkut assumes Siam's throne and ushers in government and social reforms.
1868	Chulalongkorn becomes king and continues reforming the kingdom.
1874	Thailand's first public museum opens.
1893	Chulalongkorn surrenders territory to the French.

1909   Great Britain gains control of Thai areas on the Malay Peninsula.

1917   Thailand joins France and Britain against Germany in World War I. Chulalongkorn University opens in Bangkok.

1932   Siam becomes a constitutional monarchy after a coup d'état.

1933   The Fine Arts School is founded in Bangkok.

1939   The kingdom of Siam is officially known as Thailand.

1941   Japan invades Thailand in World War II, forcing Thailand to fight against Allied powers.

1943   The Fine Arts School is renamed Silpakorn University.

1946   Bhumibol Adulyadej (Rama IX) becomes king of Thailand.

1961   Thailand's first national park—Khao Yai—is established.

1973   Student protesters lead demonstrations for democratic reforms.

1982   Musicians found the Bangkok Symphony Orchestra.

1989   The Thai government bans commercial logging.

1996   Thailand celebrates the Golden Jubilee of Rama IX's reign.

1997   Thailand's economy crashes.

2001   Thaksin Shinawatra is elected prime minister.

2002   Thailand announces plans for the world's largest HIV vaccine trial.

COUNTRY NAME Thailand

AREA 198,116 square miles (513,118 sq km)

MAIN LANDFORMS Bilauktaung Mountains, Khorat Plateau, Malay Peninsula, Phanom Dong Rak Mountains, Phetchabun Mountains

HIGHEST POINT Doi Inthanon 8,514 feet (2,595 m) above sea level

LOWEST POINT Sea level

MAJOR RIVERS Chao Phraya, Chi, Mun, Nan, Pasak, Ping, Wang, Yom

ANIMALS Asian elephant, deer, gibbon, Himalayan black bear, kouprey, leopard, rhinoceros, serow, tiger, water buffalo

CAPITAL CITY Bangkok

OTHER MAJOR CITIES Chiang Mai, Hat Yai, Ubon Ratchathani

OFFICIAL LANGUAGE Thai

MONETARY UNIT Baht. 100 satang = 1 baht.

THAI CURRENCY

Thailand's monetary unit is the baht. There are coins of one, five, and ten baht, as well as twenty-five and fifty satang. Paper currency is available in ten, twenty, fifty, one hundred, five hundred, and one thousand baht. The king is pictured on the front of every baht—coin and bill.

Thailand's flag was adopted in 1917 by King Rama VI. It consists of five horizontal stripes—red, white, blue, white, and red. The red stripes symbolize the nation, and the white stripes represent Buddhism. The wider blue band in the middle represents the Thai monarchy. Nation, religion, and monarchy all unite the Thai people.

The music for Thailand's national anthem was composed in 1932 by Phra Jenduriyang. Colonel Luang Saranuprabhandi wrote lyrics for the anthem in 1939. Thailand also has a royal anthem that honors the king. The royal anthem is played on special public occasions.

Thailand National Anthem
Thailand is the unity of Thai blood and body.
The whole country belongs to the Thai people, maintaining thus far for the Thai.
All Thais intend to unite together.
Thais love peace but do not fear to fight.
They will never let anyone threaten their independence.
They will sacrifice every drop of their blood to contribute to the nation, will serve their country with pride and prestige full of victory.

Thailand Royal Anthem
We, Your Majesty's loyal subjects,
Pay homage with deep-felt veneration,
To the supreme Protector of the Realm,
The mightiest of monarchs complete with transcendent virtues,
Under whose benevolent rule, we, Your subjects,
Receive protection and happiness,
Prosperity and peace;
And we wish that whatsoever Your Majesty may desire,
The same may be fulfilled.

For a link where you can listen to Thailand's national and royal anthems, go to vgsbooks.com.

Famous People

KING BHUMIBOL (b. 1927) Born in Cambridge, Massachusetts, King Bhumibol (Rama IX) took the throne in 1946 after the death of his older brother King Ananda. His coronation was put off for four years so that the young king could finish his higher education, with degrees in engineering and political science. The world's longest reigning monarch, King Bhumibol is also one of the most beloved by his people. He remains an effective diplomat and a symbol of national pride and unity. In addition to his political achievements, the king is a noted jazz musician and composer, an artist, a mathematician, and an award-winning sailor.

CHULALONGKORN (RAMA V) (1868–1910) Chulalongkorn became king after the death of his father, Rama IV, in 1868. Chulalongkorn, who is often considered the most revered of all Thailand's kings, helped to modernize his country. He commissioned the building of the first railway in Thailand and was the first Thai king to travel abroad. His diplomatic skills are credited with saving Thailand from colonization by European countries. Chulalongkorn was born in Bangkok.

THAWAN DACHANEE (b. 1939) Thawan Dachanee is a painter who was born in Chiang Rai. He studied at Bangkok's Arts and Crafts College, Silpakorn University, and in Amsterdam, Holland. His works have achieved international acclaim for their unique blend of classical and modern Thai elements and their expressive nature. His paintings include *Battle of Mara* and *Elephant*.

CORADO FEROCI (SILPA BHIRASRI) (1882–1962) Corado Feroci, a sculptor, is considered the father of modern art in Thailand. Feroci was born in Italy and moved to Thailand in 1923. In 1933 he helped establish the School of Fine Arts in Bangkok. He became a Thai citizen in 1944 and changed his name to Silpa Bhirasri. His works include the Democracy Monument and the statue of King Rama VI, both in Bangkok.

SOMLUCK KHAMSING (b. 1976) Born in Khon Kaen, Somluck Khamsing, a boxer, gained fame in 1996 when he became the first Thai ever to win an Olympic gold medal. In 2001 the boxer turned to another form of entertainment—acting. Khamsing accepted starring roles in a Thai television soap opera and a film about eighteenth-century Thai kickboxing legend Khanom Thom.

MONGKUT (RAMA IV) (1804–1868) Mongkut ruled as King of Siam from 1851 to 1868. As a young man, Mongkut studied Buddhist scriptures, Latin, English, science, and Western culture. During his reign, he negotiated treaties with several European countries to keep Siam independent. At the same time, he introduced Western technology to his country. His reign is marked by administrative reforms and modernization programs. Mongkut was born in Thonburi.

UPASIKA KEE NANAYON (1901–1979) Upasika Kee Nanayon, who wrote under the pen name, K. Khao-suan-luang, was one of the most important women teachers of Buddhism in modern Thailand. Born in Rajburi, Thailand, Nanayon's talks drew crowds from all over Thailand, and her poetry was widely published. Her works include *Breath Meditation* and *Looking Inward: Observations on the Art of Meditation.*

SUNTHORN PHU (1786–1855) Sunthorn Phu, born in Bangkok, is considered one of Thailand's greatest poets. As a youth, he received his education in a monastery. His early works, such as *Nirat Muang Klaeng* and *Phra Abhaimani,* attracted the attention of the royal family. King Rama II offered him a position at his court, and Sunthorn Phu soon became a favorite court poet. His poems are characterized by a mixture of romance and humor. He eventually was named Thailand's poet laureate.

QUEEN SIRIKIT (b. 1932) Queen Sirikit, born Mom Rajawongse Sirikit, spent her childhood in Bangkok. She became engaged to Prince Bhumibol in 1949, and the couple married in 1950. Since then, Queen Sirikit has been a popular figure and an ambassador for the people of Thailand. Throughout her reign, she has created and supported many social programs, including the SUPPORT Foundation, which provides education and equipment for small businesses and aid centers. She has received numerous awards for her humanitarian and conservation work.

PIRA SUDHAM (b. 1942) Pira Sudham is a writer who was born in Napo. His works describe the poor people of Thailand's northeastern region. As a boy, his parents sent him to a Buddhist monastery in Bangkok, where he learned to write. His works include *Monsoon Country* and *The Force of Karma.* Sudham, who is considered Thailand's top English-language writer, was nominated for the 1990 Nobel prize for literature.

TAO SURANARI (1772–1852) Tao Suranari, also known as Khunying Mo, was the wife of a deputy governor in the city of Khorat. In 1826 an army from Laos captured Khorat and threatened to enslave its people. Tao Suranari decided to fight back and organized some of the women to throw a party for the soldiers. They got the Laotians drunk, then killed them. In 1934 a statue of Khorat's heroine was erected in the center of town. People honor her with gifts of flowers and food, and a ten-day festival commemorates her brave deed.

TAMARINE TANASUGARN (b. 1977) Tennis player Tamarine Tanasugarn was born in the United States but moved to Thailand when she was five. Thailand's number one player, she won her first major title in 1998, four years after turning pro. In 1996 she was given the honor of carrying Thailand's flag for the 1996 Olympic Games. In addition to playing tennis professionally, Tanasugarn received a law degree from Bangkok University in 2000. She lives in Bangkok.

AYUTTHAYA Established in 1350, the historic city of Ayutthaya served as Thailand's capital until 1767. The site, which is near Bangkok, features a historical study center, the Chao Sam Phraya National Museum, palace ruins, and early Thai artifacts.

BAN CHIANG Excavations at this prehistoric village near Udon have turned up objects more than five thousand years old. Highlights include the excavation site, the museum, and the nearby Wat Phra Buddha Baht Bua Bok, a temple housing a Buddhist holy relic.

DAMNOEN SADUAK FLOATING MARKET This open-air market in Damnoen features vendors selling their wares from boats on the canals. Bargaining is common, and shoppers may find a wide variety of locally grown fresh fruits and vegetables.

GRAND PALACE The Grand Palace in Bangkok is King Rama I's most famous architectural achievement. Started in the late eighteenth century and completed in the early nineteenth century, the palace includes Wat Phra Kaeo, home to the Emerald Buddha, the most sacred Buddha image in Thailand.

KHAO YAI NATIONAL PARK Khao Yai, Thailand's first national park, features a wide variety of the country's wildlife, including Asiatic black bears and Asian elephants. Special attractions include the Heo Suwat Waterfall and the cave at Khao Rub Chang.

KO SAMUI This island in the Gulf of Thailand is a popular spot for both tourists and locals. Sandy beaches and scenic bays have made Ko Samui famous.

NATIONAL MUSEUM The National Museum in Bangkok is the largest museum in Southeast Asia. Highlights include the Thai History Gallery, the Phuttaisawan Chapel, and the Old Transportation Room.

PHUKET Visitors to Phuket can see the island's famous beaches and swim in the Andaman Sea's warm waters. A coral reef is part of the nearby Had Nai Yang National Park.

SUKHOTHAI HISTORICAL PARK Sukhothai Historical Park in Sukhothai features the Rama Khamhaeng National Museum, Wat Mahathat, and several religious shrines.

VINMAMEK MANSION MUSEUM This teakwood mansion was built in Bangkok in 1901 by King Chulalongkorn and restored in 1982 to house the royal family's memorabilia. The museum houses photographs, handicrafts, and other royal artifacts.

WAT PHRA SINGH This wat, built in Chiang Mai in the fourteenth century, houses the Phra Buddha Sihing, a highly revered Buddhist image.

Buddhism: a religion that was established by Siddhartha Gautama, known as the Buddha, in India in the sixth century B.C. Buddhism teaches that the way to enlightenment is through meditation and self-knowledge.

communism: a theory of common ownership; an economic system of government in which the government controls the means of production and distribution

Confucianism: a philosophy based on the teachings of Chinese scholar Confucius (551–479 B.C.) that spells out civil, family, and social duties

coup d'état: a sudden and decisive political action, with or without force, that usually results in a change of government

gross domestic product: the value of all goods and services produced in a country during a certain time period

Hinduism: a polytheistic religion founded by Aryans who migrated to India in the fifth century B.C. Hinduism's sacred texts are called the *Vedas*, and Hindus believe that all living things are part of the divine.

Islam: a religion based on the prophet Muhammad's teaching and founded in the seventh century A.D. Islam's holy book is the Quran, which spells out the five fundamental religious duties (or pillars) for its followers. These include believing in Allah and the prophet Muhammad, praying five times each day, giving alms to the poor, fasting during Ramadan, and making a pilgrimage to Mecca once in a lifetime.

khlong: a system of artificial canals used by the Thai to irrigate farmland and for transportation

monsoon: a seasonal wind that is often accompanied by heavy rains

nationalist: a person who feels supreme loyalty toward their nation and places a primary emphasis on the promotion of a national culture and national interests

paddies: rice fields that may be farmed either wet or dry

refugee: a person forced to flee his or her homeland due to political or economic upheaval

sakdi na: an Ayutthayan political system that distributed land among Thai males according to their social status and standing with the king

wat: a Buddhist temple or monastery

Selected Bibliography

Background Notes. October 2001.
Website: <http://www.state.gov/r/pa/ei/bgn/> **(August 2, 2002).**
This site is run by the U.S. Department of State and provides information about Thailand and other foreign countries, including the political conditions, foreign relations, and economy.

CountryWatch. June 2, 2002.
Website: <http://www.countrywatch.com/cw_country.asp?vcountry=131> **(June 2, 2002).**
CountryWatch has information about Thailand, including political history, economic conditions, environmental issues, and social customs.

Eliot, Joshua. *Bangkok and the Beaches Handbook.* Bath, England: Footprint Handbooks Ltd, 2000.
Learn more about Thailand's capital city and its world-famous resorts with this guidebook.

Eliot, Joshua, et al. *Thailand Handbook.* 3rd ed. Bath, England: Footprint Handbooks Ltd, 2001.
This guidebook covers the highlights, customs, and history of Thailand.

Europa Year World Book. Vol. 2. London: Europa Publications Ltd., 2001.
The article covering Thailand includes recent events, vital statistics, and economic information.

Eveland, Jennifer. *Frommer's Thailand.* 5th ed. New York: Hungry Minds, 2002.
This travel book offers a list of important Thai sites as well as tips for visitors.

Keyes, Charles. *Thailand: Buddhist Kingdom as Modern Nation-State.* Boulder, CO: Westview Press, 1987.
This book describes the history of the Thai government and the tensions among the social, economical, and political sectors of the nation.

Population Reference Bureau. August 2, 2002.
Website: <http://www.prb.org> **(August 2, 2002).**
The bureau offers Thailand's current population figures, vital statistics, land area, and more. Special articles cover the latest environmental and health issues that concern Thailand and other featured nations.

Statesman's Yearbook. London: Macmillan, 2001.
This resource features information about Thailand's historical events, industry and trade, climate and topography, as well as suggestions for further reading.

Thai Artists. N.d.
Website: <http://www.rama9art.org/artisan/artist/artist.html> **August 10, 2002.**
This website features information about Thai artists, both modern and historic masters, as well as links to exhibitions, galleries, and museums.

Tourism Authority of Thailand. August 1, 2000.
Website: <http://www.tat.or.th/> **August 2, 2002.**
The official Thai tourism website includes advice for visitors, historical and cultural information, and news releases.

The World Factbook. **January 1, 2001.**
Website: <http://www.cia.gov/cia/publications/factbook/geos/ez.html> **(July 20, 2002).**

This website features up-to-date information about the people, land, economy, and government of Thailand. Transnational issues are also briefly covered.

World Gazetteer. **February 15, 2002.**
Website: <http://www.gazetteer.de> **(July 20, 2002).**

The World Gazetteer offers population information about cities, towns, and places for all countries, including Thailand, along with information about their administrative divisions.

Asia-art Net
Website: <http://www.asia-art.net>
This comprehensive website offers historical and technical information about the fine arts from countries all around Asia, including Thailand.

Bangkok Post online
Website: <http://www.bangkokpost.net/>
This online version of the *Bangkok Post* features links to current news in Thailand's capital city.

Campbell, Geoffrey. *Thailand*. San Diego, CA: Lucent Books, 2001.
This book offers information about the history and culture of Thailand.

Cooper, Robert, and Nanthapa Cooper. *Culture Shock! Thailand*. Portland, OR: Graphic Arts Center Publishing, 1991.
This book covers the customs and etiquette of Thailand, such as driving rules, religious practices, and making friends.

Giles, Gail. *Breath of the Dragon*. New York: Clarion Books, 1997.
This novel tells the story of five-year-old Malila, a Thai village girl living with her grandmother. Despite being shunned by her village, Malila develops a love of her culture.

Harrison, Supenn, and Judy Monroe. *Cooking the Thai Way*. Minneapolis: Lerner Publications Company, 2003.
This book features authentic Thai recipes and facts about Thai cooking, along with historical information and a section on Thai holidays and festivals.

Ho, Minfong. *Rice without Rain*. New York: Lothrop, Lee, and Shepard, 1990.
In this novel, best friends Jinda and Ned leave their Thai village to join a political protest in Bangkok. When the protest becomes violent, the two choose to follow separate paths.

McNair, Sylvia. *Thailand: Enchantment of the World*. New York: Children's Press, 1998.
This nonfiction title offers information about the geography, history, and culture of Thailand.

———. *Bangkok*. New York: Children's Press, 1999.
This book describes the history, people, and sights of Thailand's capital city.

Richardson, Judith Benet. *First Came the Owl*. New York: Henry Holt, 1996.
In this novel, eleven-year-old Nita moves to the United States from Thailand and struggles to find a way to fit into her new life.

Thailand Life
Website: <http://www.thailandlife.com/>
This website, created and maintained by a Thai teenager, offers a glimpse of life as a youth in Thailand.

Further Reading and Websites

Tourism Authority of Thailand
Website: <http://www.tat.or.th/>

This website offers information about Thai cuisine, customs, and events, as well as facts about the most famous sights to see.

Vathanaprida, Supaporn. *Thai Tales: Folktales of Thailand.* Englewood, CO: Libraries Unlimited, 1994.

Learn more about Thailand through this collection of myths and tales. Stories cover such topics as life, the New Year, lying, animals, local legends, and tales about spirits.

vgsbooks.com
Website: <http://www.vgsbooks.com>

Visit vgsbooks.com, the homepage of the Visual Geography Series. You can get linked to all sorts of useful online information, including geographical, historical, demographic, cultural, and economic websites. The vgsbooks.com site is a great resource for late-breaking news and statistics.

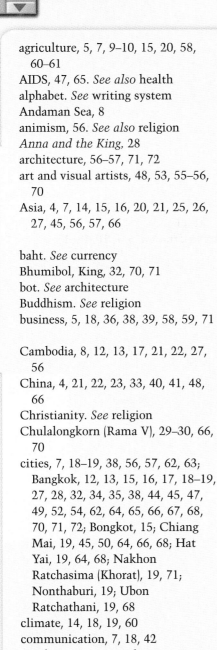

Captions for photos appearing on cover and chapter openers:

Cover: Wat Mahatat is just one of many majestic temples built during the Ayutthaya period of Thai history.

pp. 4–5 All that remains of the once magnificent city of Angkor are picturesque ruins. Ancient cities and temples draw hundreds of thousands of tourists to Thailand each year.

pp. 8–9 A storm moves in over Poda Island near the town of Krabi. Dramatic rock formations protrude from the Andaman Sea.

pp. 20–21 A relief carving on a temple wall in the ancient city of Angkor

pp. 38–39 Thai women harvest rice.

pp. 48–49 Silk umbrellas are one of Thailand's many native crafts.

pp. 58–59 A young woman creates a textile at a loom. Cloth and textiles are among Thailand's most prized exports.

Photo Acknowledgments
The images in this book are used with the permission of: © Vautier–Cazanave/Paris, pp. 4–5, 10, 15, 18–19, 20–21, 36, 38–39, 40, 41 (top), 42, 43 (bottom), 48–49, 52, 56, 57, 58–59, 64, 65; © Nevada Wier, pp. 8–9, 50; Digital Cartographics, pp. 6, 11; © Mary and Lloyd McCarthy/Root Resources, pp. 12–13, 13 (top), 24, 45, 61; © Tim Page/CORBIS, p. 14; Minneapolis Public Library, p. 16; © Claudia Adams/Root Resources, p. 17; © Nelson-Atkins Museum, p. 22; © Historical Picture Archive/CORBIS, p. 26; © Independent Picture Service, p. 29; © Hulton-Deutsch/CORBIS, p. 30; © Hulton/Archive by Getty Images, p. 32; © Bettmann/CORBIS, p. 33; © AFP/CORBIS, p. 35; © Bohemian Nomad Picturemakers/CORBIS, p. 41 (bottom); © Byron Crader/Root Resources, pp. 43 (top), 54, 55, 62; © Les Stone/CORBIS, p. 46; © Ruth Welty/Root Resources, p. 60; © Todd Strand/Independent Picture Service, p. 68.

Front Cover: © Vautier–Cazanave/Paris. Back Cover: Nasa

DATE DUE